On a Clear

C. BALAGOPAL studied economics at Loyola College, University of Madras, and then enrolled for a PhD programme (unfinished) at the University of Kerala. He joined the IAS in 1977 and worked in Manipur and Kerala before resigning in 1983 to set up a pioneering venture to make cutting-edge medical products. The enterprise today employs 1,100 people and ships products to more than fifty countries. He has retired recently and spends his time consulting, writing, reading, travelling and playing golf. He lives in Thiruvananthapuram with his wife.

Advance praise for the book

'I've been privileged to hear Bala in person as he tells his stories of his time in the IAS: he is a great raconteur. I am delighted that he has recorded these tales in *On a Clear Day You Can See India*. I read it in one go because I was having so much fun. The writing is lucid and I marvel at his wit and his ability to find the poignancy and the humour in a situation, sometimes both elements coming together in the same sentence. This volume is a delight and I hope there are more to come.'

– Abraham Verghese, author of *Cutting for Stone*

'A lyrical account of a little-known region … an enthralling read, which is by turns whimsical, humorous, poignant and piercing. Wish Bala had taken to literary work a long time ago and more must come for us from his pen.'

– Subroto Bagchi, chairman, Mindtree Limited

'A fascinating book in which the author … intelligently reflects and brings out through a series of anecdotes and events … his perceptions and views on some of the core social, political and developmental issues and problems that affect and shape the lives of people living in this remote, beautiful, wonderland called Manipur. He does this subtly and sensitively without being judgemental or patronizing.'

– Falguni Rajkumar, IAS (retd), chairman, board of governors, Rajiv Gandhi Indian Institute of Management, Shillong

On a Clear Day
You Can See India

The Little World of the District Official

C. BALAGOPAL

HarperCollins *Publishers* India

First published in India by
HarperCollins *Publishers* in 2013
A-75, Sector 57, Noida, Uttar Pradesh 201301, India
www.harpercollins.co.in

2 4 6 8 10 9 7 5 3

Copyright © C. Balagopal 2013
Photographs (cover and inserts) copyright © Ram Sinam

P-ISBN: 978-93-5029-687-5
P-ISBN: 978-93-5029-688-2

The views and opinions expressed in this book are the author's own and
the facts are as reported by him, and the publishers are not in
any way liable for the same.

C. Balagopal asserts the moral right
to be identified as the author of this work.

All rights reserved. No part of this publication may be reproduced,
stored in a retrieval system, or transmitted, in any form or by any means,
electronic, mechanical, photocopying, recording or otherwise,
without the prior permission of the publishers.

Typeset in 11/14 Minion Pro
by Jojy Philip, New Delhi 110 015

Printed and bound at
Saurabh Printers Pvt.Ltd.

This is for you, Vini
Without your encouragement,
this book would not have been completed
Without your persistence,
I would have abandoned my efforts to find a publisher
and tried to go ahead on my own

Contents

List of Abbreviations

AE	Assistant Engineer
ADC	Aide-de-camp
ADM	Additional District Magistrate
AFSPA	Armed Forces Special Powers Act
AIG	Assistant Inspector General
APP	Assistant Public Prosecutor
BDO	Block Development Officer
BRO	Border Roads Organisation
BSF	Border Security force
CEO	Chief Electoral Officer
CM	Chief Minister
CrPC	Criminal Procedure Code
CRPF	Central Reserve Police Force
CS	Chief Secretary
DAO	District Agricultural Officer
DC	Deputy Commissioner
DIG	Deputy Inspector General
DM	District Magistrate
DPO	District Planning Officer

DSP	District Superintendent of Police
DTO	District Treasury Officer
DVO	District Veterinary Officer
EC	Election Commission
ERO	Electoral Registration Officer
GPO	General Post Office
HS	Home Secretary
IAS	Indian Administrative Service
IB	Intelligence Bureau
ICS	Indian Civil Services
IGP	Inspector General of Police
IO	Intelligence Officer
IPC	Indian Penal Code
IPS	Indian Police Service
JD	Joint Director
LDC	Lower-division Clerk
MLA	Member of the Legislative Assembly
PLA	People's Liberation Army
RO	Returning Officer
SDC	Sub-deputy Collector
SDM	Subdivisional Magistrate
SDO	Subdivisional Officer
SDPO	Subdivisional Police Officer
SP	Superintendent of Police
UDC	Upper-division Clerk

Introduction

One afternoon, as I sat in my office in the square, fortress-like collectorate in Kollam finishing some pending work, I was summoned by the district collector. On entering, I was gestured into a seat in front of the large desk behind which sat the jovial incumbent. That day, however, he bore a grave expression. He looked up and with some asperity asked me about a meeting involving representatives of students' unions, transport workers' unions and the police that he had asked me to chair when he was called away on some urgent work. I explained that the meeting had been dissolved and told him the reasons that prompted me to do so. I added that all present had been told in no uncertain terms about the consequences that would follow if the students – whose unruly behaviour was the reason why we had convened – resorted to stopping buses in order to forcibly collect money for their fund. I had also cited various sections of the Indian Penal Code (IPC) and Criminal Procedure Code (CrPC) that covered their actions, a list that included dacoity, unlawful confinement, interfering with traffic on a public road, intimidation, and so on. As I warmed up and got more animated, the district collector sat back with a smile growing on his face. Finally, he said with mock exasperation: 'Balagopal, this is Kerala, not *Manipur.*'

This was a refrain that I heard often, something I only gradually came to understand. It was clearly based on the unstated premise that Manipur belonged to a region that was quite different from the rest of India, where presumably even the laws were different (which was not true), and where the administration approached issues from a very different perspective (which was quite true).

This book started out as a collection of anecdotes from my brief sojourn in Manipur nearly three decades ago. Friends who heard some of these stories (usually over a glass of rum) have often suggested that I put them together in a bound text.

So I went ahead and did just that. The person most responsible for these stories being written down is Vinita, who came into my life less than ten years ago. Over the past year, she has been persistent in her efforts to get me to write, and I am grateful to her for this, as I found myself enjoying the process of unwrapping memories that had lain undisturbed for many years in the archives of my mind. It was not so difficult to accomplish since I had some notes and diaries from those days to work with, as well as memories that were remarkably fresh despite the passage of time, and the great distance not only in physical terms from the places of their occurrence. Faces and sights and landscapes and smells and sounds and tastes from a long time ago floated up as each memory was recalled.

I am sixty as I write these words, no longer the twenty-five-year-old I was when I first went to the north-east. I think I have recounted the incidents and situations with reasonable accuracy, but it has been an effort to remember that I would have viewed many things quite differently at that age. Today, I would probably get angry about fewer issues, would accept many more things, and would advocate patience in almost everything. In those days, I too would have wanted to change things in a hurry, I too was probably not willing to compromise on many things I would let pass today, I too would not have accepted that certain things are inevitable. Then, I too would have probably been impatient with a conservative approach, saying instead that there is no time to lose, and refusing to accept that in the affairs of men, time is often the only resource we have in abundance.

I read somewhere that Wittgenstein said, 'It is difficult to know something and to act as if you did not know it.' But I cannot claim that in those days I even had an inkling of the terrible tragedy that was to unfold in later years. At that time, the north-east still appeared to be an impossibly beautiful place, with beautiful people, sparkling rivers that could turn in seconds into raging white cataracts, and dense vegetation of almost Amazonian fecundity that mastered everything that came in its path. Where the heavens opened up to make the giant rivers rise in vast sheets of water that defied description. Where nature ruled, and man was still incidental, an aberration, tolerated by nature. By stressing the particular, especially the inner processes of a typical small government office and the people involved in the stories, I have tried to resist this tendency of looking at the bigger picture, but am certain that I have not been entirely successful. I seek the reader's indulgence where such intrusions have occurred.

So, it has been doubly difficult to not only trawl through notes and memories and recapture somewhat the mood of those days as well as the drama and the tension, but also to honestly portray things as they happened, without allowing myself the benefit of not only hindsight but also age and the maturity which is supposed to go with it. I have not assigned myself any special role other than that of an observer and bit player in most of the stories, a minor protagonist in a few, and one among a few key players in a couple. In chapters where I am one of the few important players, my role would be more to bring out the inner story without which the incident cannot be understood fully.

I have not chosen this style of presentation out of any false sense of modesty or a deliberate wish to underplay my role, but perhaps, because that is probably the way I choose to view life in general, as something that happens to me, and not something that resembles the unfolding of a blueprint prepared by me. I do not recall having had a plan or 'ambition', as we called it in those days, to achieve anything particular in life. Which is why I feel like a bit of a fraud when I advise young people to have a plan, and to pursue their goal with diligence and determination.

There are many ways to approach the task of putting to words the experiences and perceptions of a time several years in the past. Each method has its advantages as well as pitfalls. I have chosen to be guided by the words of Gabriel Garcia Marquez: 'Life is not what one has lived, but what one remembers and how one chooses to tell it.'

I have adopted a semi-fictional approach for two reasons: first, my memory of some of the events and the persons involved may be in error in some details, since my notes were not very detailed and I hope the book will be forgiven that fault; second, because I wish to avoid any embarrassment for me and the protagonists of the stories by disclosing their true identities. Some people may find themselves recognizing some of the cast (including possibly themselves!) in some stories. I seek their understanding if I have erred in any detail. The fictionalized style also enables one to put in conversations which are not based on transcripts of what was actually said and helps make the narrative more readable.

The 'looking glass' picture I retain of working in Manipur all those years ago is based on this 'make-believe' quality of the way things appeared to a bemused mayang (Meitei for 'outsider'), who definitely felt like an outsider every day and every time and at every event. This comic-strip quality did not come wholly from a perception that the people were 'funny', meaning strange, which they definitely were to my 'mainland' view. It arose partly from the inexpertness born out of the unfamiliarity of the local officials with the methods of administration that had been introduced into the region not too long ago, and that had been mostly handled by outsiders, with very few local people recruited till fairly recent times. There was therefore a curious play-acting quality to many things although the players were earnest and trying to do their work diligently. Any trace of condescension that may have crept in is wholly unintended and in fact detracts from the narrative which is meant to capture this strange and beautiful world as it appeared to the eyes of a disbelieving mayang.

The book also includes a set of photographs for which I must thank my friend and the reader of an early draft of the manuscript, Ram Sinam. Though the photographs were taken during the 2000s, the landscape is still so strikingly similar to the one that I was acquainted with during the 1980s that I leapt at his offer to lend me the photographs for use in the book. Ram being a native of Manipur, with a strong attachment to his state, its culture and history, I would like to consider his offer as his stamp of approval of what my book is about.

At the end of the book, I have set out my views on the developments in the north-east and Manipur in the intervening years and have attempted to link later developments to incidents and mistakes made in the times I have written about. It is true that the root causes of the problems of the north-east must be sought in history and geography as well as in politics and administration. Since I was a very junior officer, far removed from North Block and the state secretariat, with very little idea of policy, I have depicted things as they were seen and negotiated by me during my brief stint there and tried to bring out the way in which the administration contends with issues at the ground level, far from the legislatures and high courts, in distant district and subdivisional headquarters. The seeds of some of the future problems of the north-east were fatefully sown in the events leading up to the 1980 general elections, and the tragic harvest we have reaped since then was in many cases foreseen by young officers. I had a ringside view of some of these developments as they unfolded in parts of Manipur.

I do not claim any special knowledge or expertise on the problems of the region and indeed have not read too widely from the considerable literature that has accumulated on the subject today. Despite these inadequacies on my part, this book will lead to a better understanding of the problems of the region, and from that should flow better policies.

I have noticed a tendency among Indian commentators to refer to the north-east mostly in terms of its complex ethnic mosaic, stressing the tribal differences, their conflicts, territorial overlaps and the manner in which tribal equations have influenced the democratic processes. There is thus an understated but patronizing approach that leads to a loss of valuable insights and perspective, resulting in flawed analysis of root causes.

Any discussion on the region should take into account its history, geography, economics and other factors, in addition to the undoubtedly important role of tribe and village community. Stressing only one or two of these factors will lead to a partial view of what is a complex reality. A system approach compels us to consider all the possible factors that are likely to have an impact on outcomes. Such a method is needed when one approaches the question of the economic, political and social development of the north-east.

While serious students of the affairs of the north-east have started to move in this direction, mainstream national media, and consequently, mainstream public opinion, appears to still be mired in the clichés and images of the past. There is still very little travel to the north-east from the rest of India, although the number of people from the region travelling to other parts of India to study or get medical treatment has grown significantly. Young north-easterners are finding increasing avenues of employment in emerging sectors such as call centres, airlines, hotel and tourism, etc., where their easy command over English and their comfort with Western modes of dress and behaviour equip them to do better than their counterparts from the mainland.

More people, especially the young, from other parts of the country travelling to the north-east is the best way of improving the understanding of the problems of the region and the perspectives of its people. Neither will such travel threaten the locals – in the sense of their feeling swamped and 'assimilated'. Already, the powerful but less evident forces of globalization and marketization are at work, creating a pan-Indian identity that Pavan K. Varma has studied in his excellent work *Being Indian*. The north-east is not going to be immune from such forces and their impact. Much that is special and unique about the region may be lost in the process. But much that needs change will also undergo positive transformation.

But before we begin with me recounting my experiences in this cosy little corner of the country, I would like to give you an idea about the socio-political scenario in Manipur and the historical forces that shaped it, as also a glimpse into my own life and the important characters (and more importantly, the IAS denominations and hierarchies) that populate the text you are about to read.

The Stage

Manipur is one of the 'seven sisters' that comprise the north-eastern part of India, the large inverted triangle connected to India by a narrow strip that is squeezed between Bangladesh and Nepal. Bounded on the north and north-east by China, to the west by Bangladesh, and in the east by Myanmar, this region is defined by the mighty Brahmaputra flowing from east to west (forming the Assam valley) and the towering Himalayas to the north that then curve to the south to merge with the mountains of Burma, and the north–south oriented ranges of the Naga hills.

Manipur covers an area of 12,000 sq. km, and is mostly mountainous with a large flat valley in the centre surrounded by a series of mountain ranges. (The references to 'valley' in the subsequent chapters pertain to this valley in the Central District.) In the 1970s, the state was divided into five districts which were simply named North, South, East, West, and Central. A tiny portion to the west – adjacent to the Silchar valley at a place called Jiribam – was attached to Central District. Today, the number of districts has gone up to ten. It is interesting to recall that Manipur was a district in the erstwhile Assam state, and was administered by a deputy commissioner. In fact, the DC's residence was later converted into the chief minister's (CM) official residence.

Being a princely state, Manipur had all the trappings of princely rule, including palaces, a fort, and a colourful history of battles with neighbours, and a ruling class – earlier entirely drawn from among the Meitei community, who mostly lived in the central valley – with a severely delineated pecking order. They professed a Vaishnavite Hinduism, having been converted less than 200 years earlier in one of the few known cases of Hindu proselytization. The ruler embraced Hinduism first, and then with the dirigisme practised by most rulers, wanted his people to follow suit. To aid him in this task, he imported Vaishnavite preachers from Orissa. They obviously did their job very well, because they also succeeded in imprinting on what was till then a casteless society all the structures of the chaturvarna system – of the deadly, exclusionist variety – with a thoroughness that would have been appreciated by Manu himself. Caste soon came to govern all the important transactions of this isolated society, and caste marks became very prominent.

To people like me, with parents who had dropped their caste names in response to the modernizing impulses that swept through parts of India in the first half of the twentieth century, it was at first amusing, and later as I got to understand the people better, somewhat tragic to see this ersatz caste system, so carefully tended by people who were unaware of it not too long back.

This strange system nurtured under hothouse conditions had some unintended consequences. The Meiteis, who ruled Manipur till the advent of Indian independence, naturally felt themselves superior to the people of the hills – such as the Nagas, Mizos, and Kukis – who were classified as belonging to the Scheduled Tribes and became eligible for various benefits under the affirmative action policies followed after 1947. The benefits included reservation of seats in UPSC appointments, which led to many from among them getting selected to the IAS, Indian Police Service (IPS) and other higher civil services. By haughtily refusing to be classified as Scheduled Tribes, the Meiteis missed out on these opportunities and found themselves having to serve those from the hill tribes.

Another consequence was the tension between tribal society – with its essentially homogeneous, undifferentiated and unstratified character – and the heterogeneous, differentiated and stratified 'Hindu' society of the Meiteis. Unlike the rest of the tribal communities in India, the tribes of the north-east did not get assimilated and did not acquire a mix of traits through contact. They thus retained their distinctive Palaeo-Mongoloid character, which sets them apart from the people of the rest of India.

The decades after Independence saw Delhi tinkering with the delicate mosaic that was the north-east, in an unwise and vain attempt to pander to every local pressure and pull. What started out as a single state, Assam, was broken into Assam and Union Territories, the latter being directly administered by Delhi. This led to agitations for statehood, which was granted reluctantly. Thus Manipur, Nagaland, Mizoram, etc., which were districts of the erstwhile Assam state, became full-fledged states with all the administrative structures that entailed. In practice, this meant that the erstwhile DC's bungalow became the CM's bungalow, the DC's office the secretariat, and so on. Very soon, large offices and quarters were built, consuming large amounts of scarce resources that were urgently needed to cater to more pressing needs. New townships were laid out, mostly to serve the burgeoning numbers of officials who needed accommodation. Fleets of vehicles bought to ferry the officials on their endless 'official' tours clogged the streets of the new towns, while the more urgently needed freight trucks remained in shortage, and mostly in private hands, earning freight rates that were much higher than in the rest of the country. Manipur had a population barely equal to that of a normal sized district in India. One can begin to imagine the cost of an entire state administration having to be borne by such an unviable entity.

The creation of states based on tribal and ethnic identity did not have the intended effect in the north-east, and internecine strife and disputes increased steadily. Growing corruption, political opportunism and a readiness to turn to the military at the slightest provocation, all contributed to the worsening of the situation. The insensitivity of the local administration to local concerns like the influx of outsiders worsened the situation.

Two facts about the north-east stand out: the economic backwardness and the insurgency that has spread to almost all parts of the region. In 1947, Assam had one of the highest per capita incomes of all states in the country. By the first decade of the present century, it ranked fourth from the bottom. Huge amounts of money have been poured into the region in the name of economic development over the years, but there is little improvement to be seen on the ground.

Dissatisfaction among the youth has fuelled the insurgency and has kept the pot simmering, despite a massive increase in the deployment of the military and paramilitary forces in the region from the times in which the narrative is set. However, there seems to have been little improvement in the situation – a clear indication that a military solution will not work. The Armed Forces Special Powers Act (AFSPA) that empowers the armed forces but renders the locals soft targets has been another point of concern.

However, historian D.D. Kosambi said, 'India is a country of long survivals.' Students of Indian society and history have been struck repeatedly by the presence of 'survivals' at every level; Manipur is a fascinating case.

The Cast

I am an ex-IAS officer who later turned to business and industry. At the time of the incidents narrated in the book, I was in my mid-twenties, having recently been selected to the IAS. I was born in Kollam, Kerala; did my schooling in Lawrence School, Lovedale; and read economics at Loyola College, University of Madras, where I completed my BA and MA. After a brief spell of being enrolled in a PhD programme (unfinished) at the University of Kerala, I joined the IAS in 1977.

As the son of a rubber plantation manager with a British company, I grew up in a family that had produced doctors, engineers, teachers and lawyers, but no government official for the past several generations. Handicapped by not having gone to Delhi University, I did not gain the understanding of the importance of the IAS in the governance of the country, and therefore arrived in Mussoorie with little idea of what to expect. In fact, before leaving for the Lal Bahadur Shastri (LBS) Academy of Administration, I went with a friend to the latter's brother who happened to be a senior IAS officer in Trivandrum. My question, to the vast amusement of my friend's brother, was: 'Do we really have to take the vast amount of clothes mentioned in the list?' The answer was brief: 'Take along just the bare essentials. The rest will be provided by enterprising fellows like Hari & Co. at Mussoorie, who will have sized you up before you have clambered off the bus or taxi at the academy!'

While many of the new arrivals at the LBS Academy appeared to know each other and were gaily exchanging greetings and yells of recognition, I had to wend my way to my allotted room since I did not know anyone. Before long, I had made several friends from among the newcomers, a process that was helped along by the transformation that appeared to have taken place in my disposition – the non-drinking, chain-smoking, studious Bala suddenly threw off his past identity like a snake shedding its skin and transformed into someone entirely different. The first step was to open a bottle of Old Monk (which thereafter became a staple for the duration at the academy, occasionally being replaced by whichever brand was available, and even by jerry cans of 'chhang' when all normal options were exhausted). The second was to correct the mistake of my university days, when I had shunned the company of girls to follow an almost monastic life in the mistaken idea that I needed to concentrate on the higher task of acquiring learning and scholarship.

The other protagonists of the narrative are, as may be expected, the usual cast of officials who feature in any story based on the happenings in any district in India. They start with the district collector, a position that was renamed 'deputy commissioner' in Manipur. This functionary is easily the most powerful and visible official of the government in India. He enjoys territorial jurisdiction over the revenue district, which normally has a population of about two million. At last count, there were 600 districts in India, with new ones being created almost every month, as states struggle to contend with competing demands from powerful local interests (including instances where competing castes and parties clamour for districts to be named after their leaders).

The additional district magistrate – or ADM, as he is more commonly referred to – is the other important district official. At that time (I am not really sure about the current situation) in Manipur, especially in Central District, the ADM was an IAS officer too, indicating the importance attached by the state government to this district. The ADM, while nominally the second-in-command of the district, also had important appellate powers relating to revenue matters. Hence, quite a bit of his time was occupied with cases and court work.

Then came the subdivisional officer (SDO) or sub-collector as he is called in some parts of the country. This is another important post, having territorial jurisdiction and wielding considerable magisterial powers. This was usually about half of a district, although there are several districts that are divided into three. The interesting point to note here is that while the SDO is subordinate to the district collector in revenue matters, in his role as subdivisional magistrate (SDM), he is not subordinate to the district magistrate (DM). An appeal against an order of the SDM has to be filed before the district judge! The SDM in fact hears cases under more sections of the IPC than the DM, with wide powers under what are referred to as the 'preventive' sections of the IPC and CrPC.

The rest of the staff at the SDO's office include the superintendent, usually of the rank of tahsildar or deputy tahsildar (referred to in Manipur as sub-deputy commissioner); a couple of upper-division clerks (UDCs); a few lower-division clerks (LDCs); assistants; and the omnipresent and unusually named peons, of whom there was always a copious supply as there was need for much fetching and carrying, not just of files, but of important work accessories such as wads of paan, packs of cigarettes, steaming hot tumblers of tea, etc. A key member of the office team is the confidential assistant who also doubles as the stenographer. This person ends up being the 'eyes and ears' of the SDO who invariably does not speak the local language and is ignorant of the highly nuanced features of the local administrative set-up.

The other powerful arm of government represented at the district level is the police. The district superintendent of police (DSP) headed this branch and exercised great power over the affairs of the district. It was not uncommon for there to exist hostility between the DC and the DSP. Over the years, the balance appears to have shifted inexorably towards the police, as politicians find it politic to keep the police in good humour. This has had the unfortunate effect of undermining that excellent principle of British India – that of exercising magisterial control over the uniformed services, which had the salutary effect of ensuring that a check was exercised over the 'power' of the police to use violent means to enforce the law.

The rest of the district administration these days appears to operate in self-contained silos, with a district head at the top and a full complement of staff. These include the district medical officer, district veterinary officer (DVO), district agricultural officer (DAO), district planning officer (DPO), and district treasury officer (DTO). In earlier times, while the department headed by each of these officers was functionally independent, the DC was captain of the team at the district level. This undefined yet important role served to help coordinate the working of the various offices in the district, far away from the gaze of the state capital. In fact, it used to be said that all powers not expressly assigned to any functionary in the district is vested in the DC. In other words, the DC represented the authority and majesty of the government. This meant that the protocol manuals stipulated that the DC will preside over any function held in the district, irrespective of the status of the others attending the function.

The other important member of the cast is the SDO's driver. This person serves many more roles than just that of piloting the rickety vehicle assigned to the SDO. Like the confidential assistant, he too is the 'eyes and ears' of the SDO and can be a valuable lieutenant in many a situation. Usually, if the SDO is from another state and does not speak the local language, the driver also serves as the interpreter, in which role his influence grows proportionately.

It is interesting to picture this complex machinery of the district administration working every day in over 600 districts, churning out reports, issuing certificates, assigning land, evicting encroachers, verifying survey records – doing all the quotidian tasks of governance and administration and matters of direct concern to the ordinary citizen through the length and breadth of this huge country. Like the autonomous nervous system of the human body managing myriad tasks with little intervention from the brain, these tasks get done with hardly any superintendence, guidance or control from the top. Indeed, it is well-nigh impossible to imagine how such a mammoth number of little tasks can ever be done in a centralized manner.

So, now that we know all there is to know about the conditions as they were in the north-east around the time of my stint there, we will dive into the rest of this narrative from the big board into the pond that is the district and see what happens in that little world. We will come across some strange and interesting sights and encounters and try to get an even clearer understanding of the people, by seeing them go about the ordinary business of their work and lives in minor government offices and outside in a distant corner of this country.

India Point

The daily routine of an IAS probationer is something many look back on with fondness as they progress in their careers. Probation is a period during which young recruits have little to do, are not held accountable for anything, are treated with consideration even by senior IAS officers, and find their visits to various government offices treated by those hosting them as an event. While there are periods when they are put through formal structured training, much of the time is spent being 'attached' to a particular office or officer. What this generally means is that the officer to whom one is attached does not have a clear idea about what to do with the probationer and the situation ends up with the former having to suffer being shadowed by a respectful and attentive young probationer throughout the day.

As an IAS probationer, I did not have much to do except tag along with the deputy commissioner as he went about his work. I often wondered how people in the various offices I visited felt about working under the serious scrutiny of an enthusiastic intern, with pencil and notebook held at the ready to jot down valuable observations.

The DC I was attached to appeared to enjoy having me around, probably as comic relief. In remote Tamenglong, headquarters of West District, very little happened to disturb the placid surface of life as one day quietly slipped into the next. Any diversion was therefore probably welcome, even if it was in the form of a young chap tailing him, determined to make a good impression.

But by the second week, I had come to expect something out of the ordinary every day from our unusual DC, despite his laid-back attitude and jaunty spirit. Although born to a traditional conservative south Indian family, he had been educated in Delhi and had been brought up in a liberal atmosphere. He had been practically brought up by an uncle, who was a senior officer in the Indian Army. This took him to many remote parts of the country during his childhood and adolescence, exposing him to many cultures and influences, and left him with an abiding interest in and love for natural history. Like many bright young people of those days, he too ended up writing the UPSC examinations and being selected to the IAS.

The DC had a wry and sardonic sense of humour, wrapping everything he said in a riddle, leaving it to the listener to figure out exactly what he meant. Every encounter with him left others puzzled, with their expressions suggesting there was something they wished to get clarified but could not quite decide what! He saw the comic side of everything, and once you understood that, it was amusing to see things through his eyes. He appeared to be laughing at everyone (including himself) and everything, but not in an unkind way. That seemed to be his way of making sense of his situation.

He was single and appeared to be a confirmed bachelor, quite content with this state of affairs, which was evident and reflected in the beautiful home he kept. His bookshelves spoke much about the man, with Camus and Kafka keeping company with Kazantzakis, Gerald Durrell, Shaw and Salim Ali. A few framed photographs on the walls – of people and vistas and birds – revealed a photographer of some ability.

Even the most ordinary question or even a greeting elicited an apparently unrelated counter-question or observation as a response, baffling the listener. Enigmatic queries in files had members of the staff scratch their heads in perplexity as he delighted in the ambiguous and the grey areas between certainties. It could be said that he inhabited a world of pastel colours, with no sharp outlines, where ambiguity reigned, and where everyone spoke in riddles.

After completing a nine-month training programme at the National Academy of Administration at Mussoorie, I was one of the two probationers allotted the state of Manipur for field training, and had been assigned to this delightful man for the next few weeks.

I was born into a middle-class family in Kerala, where my father was employed in a British plantation company. I spent my childhood in tea and rubber plantations in the Western Ghats, and my schooling, as a result, was mostly in a residential school up in the mountains near Ooty. The eldest of three boys, I grew up with an overdeveloped sense of responsibility, which made me do things no one had ever called upon me to do, and prevented me from doing many things that no one ever asked me not to do and which I am sure would have made my childhood more enjoyable.

After a very 'physical' schooling in which I learnt to play every game and sport with some degree of competence, at university I was at a crossroads. Unlike some of my more sensible classmates who turned to the business of having a good time and sowing their wild oats, I threw myself heart and soul into academic pursuits, resulting in my excelling at academics. I won every medal and prize in sight, to the great satisfaction of my parents. I also took to smoking with some determination, going through three to four packs a day – probably my only sign of rebellion during my college days!

It was only when I joined the IAS and reached Mussoorie that something that had been bottled up inside me burst and I finally came to understand that there is a time and place for everything; that one must do what one must when one must! Suffice it to say that I sowed my wild oats when I was twenty-four. Bunking a lecture was a gesture, and act of freedom, a sensation I had never experienced before. It was a heady feeling when, while making my way to the academy gate, I passed the course director on his way in and I walked on after courteously exchanging greetings with him, knowing that he would stand there looking after me in perplexity. My attendance at lectures was abysmal and my locker (more aptly described as a pigeonhole) was stuffed with notices asking for my explanation, which I ignored with glee. Evenings were spent at Whispering Windows, a bar popular with others like me, or in the room where the room orderly, Ram Singh, would have got ready a fresh bottle of Old Monk, two glasses and jug of water. By 9 p.m., the bottle would be empty, and we would make it to the mess just in time to grab a plate of the mediocre fare on offer, and I would head for the table where the girls – who always made room for me and never uttered words of reproof to me, mind you – sat. The food eaten, I would repair with my mug of coffee to the lounge and ask the man in charge of the gramophone booth to put on Siddheshwari Devi's '*Jao balam naahi bol*'. It was then that I would, for the first time in the day, feel free from the desire to cram as much activity as I could into each hour and allow the golden voice to pour over me like soothing warm water. My head would clear up and I would follow the lament of the woman that her man does not speak to her.

Being posted to Manipur was therefore not the unmitigated disaster it was for most others, who then spent most of their waking hours planning how to spend as little time of their careers as possible in Manipur. While I did not look too far ahead, I could see myself enjoying my stint in the state, however long it lasted. A different place, new people, new experiences. That's what I thought then. My living it up in Mussoorie naturally had its impact on my professional life – I slipped in the official ranking by several places. I vaguely recall well-meant advice from a member of the academy faculty that if I did not pull up my socks, this slipping would affect my career prospects. But I was having such a good time sinning that I preferred to leave all thoughts of repentance to the future.

I was posted to West District to do a stint attached to the deputy commissioner there. This meant I had to accompany the DC as he went about his work. I guess I was supposed to observe how the DC handled various situations and also study the working of the district administration. I was accommodated at the inspection bungalow adjacent to the DC's, to which I would walk over to every morning to have breakfast with him. The food at any inspection bungalow is usually execrable, which I had begun to tire of almost from the first day there! For the rest of the day, I just had to tag along with the DC. So the sight of me following the DC and his shaggy hill dog Domingo soon became a common spectacle to the local people.

One day after breakfast, which consisted of parathas and curd and pickle with toast and butter and jam followed by steaming coffee, the DC informed me that the programme for the day was an inspection of a pineapple project. He added that he would try to show me India Point. Knowing better than to ask what we would see there, as that would merely have elicited another inscrutable reply from the laconic DC, I followed him and Domingo into the jeep, which already seated another probationer and a lambu (means tall, but here a term used for helpers assigned to me and other IAS officers by the office to help with the housework). The uniformed driver switched on the revolving light and we were off in a cloud of dust.

Only those who have travelled in the rear of a jeep that has the seats facing each other will understand the marked lack of interest in small talk in that part of the vehicle as the occupants hang on to anything that offers a handhold to prevent them being thrown off at every curve. The presence of a large shaggy canine in our midst did not help matters. Each sharp turn found the four occupants of the rear on the same side of the vehicle, wedged firmly together in a tangle of coats, trousers, arms, bushy tail, cold wet snout, etc., with sides being reversed as the vehicle was hurled around the next curve. The DC prattled on, pointing out passing flora, his attention especially drawn to varieties of orchid, about which he seemed to have considerable knowledge.

We had been travelling thus for about an hour and had been shaken and stirred till we were seeing three and four images. Just as we plucked up the courage to request an urgent halt on grounds of extreme distress, the jeep started to slow down and finally came to a halt on a grassy knoll. We staggered out and painfully went about the process of rearranging and stretching our dislocated and cramped limbs.

The DC meanwhile had tramped up the slope to a fenced area bearing a large sign which declared 'IHADP Pineapple Plantation'. There was a gate of sorts in the fence, and the path continued its precipitous course up the slope till it disappeared over a rise. We had in the meantime sorted out which limb belonged to whom to the satisfaction of all, especially of Domingo who appeared to be the most fastidious about the process. He walked up the slope with vast dignity, pausing to salute a bush in the time-honoured canine manner while we followed at a respectful distance. The DC declared that he would like to see the plantation. The block development officer (BDO) and his clerk who were waiting for us at the spot began to perspire although it was not such a warm day. They protested that it would be taxing for the DC to climb the steep slope, but to no avail, since one of the few joys in the DC's life was hiking in the mountains in pursuit of his hobbies: birdwatching and photography.

The BDO's warning regarding the steepness of the slope was not far off the mark and we were soon huffing and puffing. The DC, on the other hand, bounded up the track like a mountain goat and was soon lost to sight over the rise we saw from the road. A few minutes later, we too crested the convex rise and found the DC seated on a rock, binoculars to his eyes, as he intently studied something on a tree some distance from where we were. Gesturing to us to keep silent, he peered through the field glasses intently for a minute or two more, and beckoning us closer, invited us to take a look. As I peered through the powerful glasses at the wildly pitching landscape caused by unsteady hands, with trees and rocks swaying and yawing crazily, the DC whispered, 'That's a Manipur bush quail, a rare bird, on the endangered list, Manipur being the only place in the subcontinent where it is found. Not so easy to spot, and one of the few I have seen in quite some time. I'll show it to you in Salim Ali's book when we get back in the evening.' He rightly guessed that I did not get a good look at the bird, having seen something scuttle under the bushes on hearing us.

He then turned to the BDO and said, 'Okay, my friend. Let us take a look at the pineapple plantation.' Then, pointing to me and my fellow probationer, he added, 'By the way, my memory isn't what it used to be and I've forgotten, so please inform these young colleagues what IHADP stands for.' The BDO seemed to struggle for air, and we thought he was in distress. He began to say, 'Intensive ... intensive ... intensive ...'

'That makes three *I*s, my friend,' the DC said genially, 'but I recall only one *I*. What do the rest of the letters stand for? After all, you and your colleagues here are drawing your pay and expenses thanks to the funds flowing from this project.' He turned and winked at us as he spoke, but we did not detect any levity in either his tone or his expression. Neither obviously did the BDO, because there was no answering smile on his face. Not getting any answer, the DC went on. 'All right. Can you explain what's so "intensive" about this project? The pineapple project, I mean,' he added with a smile that did not reach his eyes. The BDO continued to act stricken by some malady that deprived him of speech or movement and stared fixedly at the ground while his assistant looked into the middle distance.

The DC now asked quietly, 'And now we come to the interesting part. Where are the pineapples, the reason why we are here?'

We were all a little confused, thinking he referred to the fruit which he wished to consume during the halt, but soon realized that he was referring to the plantation. The BDO looked even more pained as his eyes continued to bore a hole in the ground. His gaze was so fixed that we found ourselves staring at the same spot too, as if expecting something to erupt through the surface. The DC walked over to where the cleared plot ended, and looked at the forest beyond. He traced the boundary, tapping at the bushes with his sturdy walking stick as he paced the entire area. Returning to where the hapless BDO stood, the DC said, 'I have been around the entire plot and the so-called "pineapple plantation" mentioned on the board. I did not find a single pineapple. Nor do I see any evidence of any pineapples having been planted here. The file shows that you have declared that a pineapple plantation has been established here, and on that basis you have drawn substantial sums of money and provided accounts for the same. These appear to have been verified and endorsed and recommended by the assistant engineer (AE) of the block. My inspection reveals that the entire matter is a pack of lies and a fabrication, and therefore a fraud. You are hereby placed under suspension. You will immediately return to your headquarters and arrange to hand over charge to your deputy, and await further disciplinary action. Have I made myself clear?'

The unfortunate BDO nodded, while his assistant – who did not appear to speak English but dimly comprehended what was happening – continued to examine the surrounding vegetation closely, for want of anything better to do. The DC waited while the BDO climbed into his jeep, followed by his clerk, and the vehicle slowly made its way down the winding road.

The DC briskly walked down the steep slope to the road, and instead of climbing into the waiting jeep, walked on up the road. The suddenness of the action taken against the BDO had caught us unawares, and we were still pondering over what we had witnessed. Almost without thinking, we too got down and followed the DC to where he was headed.

I looked around me. The hills rose on all sides, but the ground in front of us fell away to a deep valley and we could hear the faint, low-pitched roar of distant cataracts as a river thundered through some narrow gorge. Beyond the valley, the hills rose and fell in a series of parallel ranges.

The DC called us closer to where he stood, leaning on the sturdy walking stick he always carried when on tour. His hat was set at a jaunty angle, a feather sticking out. His untidy goatee sprinkled with a few grey strands framed a humorous mouth with slightly protruding teeth.

His face was relaxed once again, the hardness that had crept in during the exchange with the BDO having disappeared almost completely. He tickled Domingo behind his ear, setting the giant dog's tail wagging in huge swathes. He beckoned us closer and turned to look out over the vista spread before us.

He pointed with the walking stick and said, 'East is in that direction. There lie Ukhrul and Burma.' The stick swung precisely ninety degrees and he continued, 'To the north lie Nagaland and Assam.' The stick, which by now had assumed magical powers and appeared to have become a giant compass needle, now swung 180 degrees to point in the opposite direction. The DC said, 'To the south lies Central District, then South District, and then Burma.' He paused and turned slowly to face west.

The sun had still some way to go before it reached its zenith, and we looked along our foreshortened shadows. The magic walking stick quivered slightly, as if responding to distant magnetic impulses as the DC went on in an expressionless voice: 'And there, to the west, my young friends, on a clear day, you can see India!'

The Deputy Commissioner, the Parish Priest and John the Baptist

🦅

We had been on the hiking trail for most of the day, having started after an early meal as was the custom in the north-east. The path ran along steep hillsides that were densely forested and covered with equally thick underbrush, making progress difficult. In many places, a lambu had to swing his daw (a scimitar-like machete) to cut a path through the undergrowth. Where the obstacle was a bamboo thicket, we either had to skirt it or wait while the lambus hacked a path through. Freshly cut bamboo has razor sharp edges that can easily rip flesh, so we had to be doubly careful.

The DC, belonging to that minority of the human race who believed that humans were designed for walking long distances, ambled along with easy strides. He was wearing sturdy walking shoes, baggy corduroys, a khaki shirt and loose jacket and appeared quite comfortable, chatting as he walked, pointing out things of passing interest. He was an avid amateur botanist and birdwatcher with a fair knowledge of the flora and fauna of the region, and so his running commentary was both informative and entertaining. As usual, he was accompanied by his big, shaggy dog, of indeterminate parentage. The dog clearly enjoyed these treks and was in his element running ahead of the group, barking at sundry creatures and stopping to examine a strange scent, sometimes with his hair standing on end. As the sun rose higher in the sky, the dog's pace would slacken, till he was reduced to panting in the middle of the pack, beseeching us with liquid eyes for some rest and a drink of cool water, his tongue hanging out of the side of his mouth.

Equipped with tennis sneakers which, after the first hour or so, proved themselves unsuited for the purpose, I marched along, trying to give the impression of being a hardy mountain type for whom such a trek was mere saunter. The path was wet and the clayey soil turned the ground underfoot into a veritable skating rink, which we had to negotiate by grabbing at the bushes and bamboos on either side in the manner of ski poles, our feet slithering and scrabbling for a grip on the treacherous ground. It was difficult to preserve my dignity in the face of this challenge and these efforts were observed with much amusement by the accompanying staff members, who had among them the local SDO, the sub-deputy collector (SDC), several lambus bearing boxes of files and our personal effects, and a 'red blanket' (a red blanket was awarded to a villager signifying that he was a person who kept village records) from the village where we were to camp that evening.

After a couple of hours, our jackets off and draped limply over the shoulders, and our shirts sticking to our bodies, we were exhausted. The DC conferred with the SDO and the column halted where there was some shade. A small group of villagers waiting for us materialized out of the forest. One of them swung a daw and the bunch soon produced several tall mugs fashioned out of the sections of a bamboo pole. Into each, another poured a frothing whitish liquid out of a gourd slung on his back. This was offered to the DC who took one, as did the SDO. We young trainee officers were then invited to take one each. Before we took a swig, the DC explained that this was zu, a kind of rice beer favoured by the local people and considered very refreshing. The others politely refused saying they did not consume alcohol, to the astonishment of the party and the villagers, who broke into animated chatter at this information. It was left to me to retrieve the honour of the new recruits into the civil administration, and I had a mouthful to find that I enjoyed the drink which tasted a bit like buttermilk. Polishing off my 'glass', I extended it to the man with the gourd, indicating that I wanted more. This was greeted with animation and after two more refills, I felt ready for another day's trek, while my colleagues wondered whether they would end up having to carry me before the day was over! The DC observed wryly that I had made up for the other trainees, and on the other hand gave them quizzical glances at their abstemiousness.

The zu having been consumed, the march resumed and we soon spotted a gathering of people ahead. As we approached, the waiting group burst into song, conducted by one among their number with gusto. We could decipher English words sung not unmusically, and soon realized that we were being serenaded with a welcome song composed in honour of the visit of the DC and his entourage. A visit by the DC was uncommon enough to warrant festivities and special ceremonies in these parts. Behind the village choir was a banner that proclaimed, 'WELLCOME MISTER R. NATH IAS, DEPTY COMMR, TAMENGLONG by Songang school teacher'. The artist who had made the banner and included the helpful information that he was the schoolteacher had not omitted to sign his name prominently. The banner indicated that his students were likely to have an imaginative approach to spelling and grammar.

The welcome song eventually ended and, as was customary, we applauded their efforts with enthusiastic and sustained clapping. There was much smiling for a while. Then the village headman – who was probably over sixty-five – clad in the official 'red blanket' stepped forward and delivered a long and impressive speech in the local dialect. This was greeted with nods and smiles and occasional chuckles by most listeners, with the DC and the four visitors smiling blankly while the words poured forth in a torrent, occasionally interrupted by a bout of coughing or hawking ending with gurgles as phlegm was spat out in large dollops. Finally, urged along by warning mutterings from the SDO, who was from those parts, the 'red blanket', as these worthies were rather uncharitably referred to in official parlance, ended his speech and sat down, overcome by another paroxysm of violent coughing and hawking.

The DC replied with a shorter speech, which on the evidence of the elaborate translation by the SDO, turned out to have been a masterpiece in brevity, capturing in a few sentences what took the SDO much longer to explain. The honours having been done, the enlarged group moved on, leaving the choir behind, which proceeded to render the other songs in its repertoire – mostly popular rock 'n' roll numbers, interspersed with hymns and carols. The singing was tuneful and well coordinated. Soon, we were in the village which comprised the typical huts made of bamboo and mud with wooden frames, and topped with thatch. The entrances were low, and there were no windows, just an opening under the eaves for the smoke to escape. The interiors were dark and smelly and appeared to be shared by adults, children as well as animals, usually pigs and dogs, with a rare chicken or two. We were shown to the hut we were to share for the night. It had been swept clean, and the human and animal occupants had been assigned alternative quarters for the night. We did not have much difficulty in guessing the identity of the recently evicted inmates as there was evidence in the form of strong odours and more substantial evidence that had obviously escaped the cursory cleaning the hut had been subjected to.

After washing our hands and faces at a large pot set outside our hut, we were invited to the headman's hut for dinner. NM, a devout Muslim, thoughtfully eyed the pigs that appeared to have the run of the place and shuddered when the ear-splitting caterwaul that accompanies the killing of a pig shattered the mountain quiet. The rest of us looked nervously around, trying to imagine the repast our hosts had planned for us, having heard tales of the varied fare that could be expected. Only the DC appeared nonchalant, though he was a strict vegetarian.

We were all seated around a blazing fire that helped to keep the mountain chill away but which also emitted billowing clouds of smoke that did not always rise in a straight column to the top. Assorted glasses and tin tumblers that had only been roughly rinsed had replaced the far more hygienic do-it-yourself bamboo glasses we had used on the trail. Our glasses were filled with a clear fluid from a large jerry can with a wooden stopper. As the glasses were raised tentatively to waiting lips, the DC cautioned me as I appeared the most eager to sample the drink: 'Take it slowly, CB. This stuff is no doubt made from rice like zu, but it is a distilled product called sekmai. It burns with a blue flame, being practically pure alcohol!'

While the other three gingerly sipped at their glasses, I put my head back and tossed the drink down the hatch. The liquid burned its fiery way down my throat and I grinned and extended my tumbler for a refill, to appreciative exclamations of the gathering. The contents of the refilled tumbler disappeared like its predecessor, to more encouragement and shouts of approval. I was by now grinning from ear to ear, and ignoring the DC's warning look, extended my glass for more.

While the men went about the serious business of drinking and discussing village accounts and petty disputes, the women got the dinner ready. Soon, plates heaped with rice were placed before each guest. A large bowl with large slabs of fried pork and another with chicken cut into little pieces that made it impossible to say which part of the bird a piece came from, were passed around. While NM avoided the pork, we took pieces of pork dripping with melted fat. Taking the cue from our hosts, we set to with a will, since we were ravenous after the long, hot and sweaty trek during the day. The sticky rice characteristic of those parts tasted quite good once one got used to its texture, and we found the unmarinated pork pieces quite tasty when taken with the rice. Whether it was the taste of the food, my hunger or the effect of the sekmai, I was not sure, but I ended up consuming rather more than I thought myself capable of. Even the others, without the assistance of sekmai, appeared to have done justice to the meal. Rinsing our hands without soap did not remove any of the grease, which meant we had to go to sleep with sticky, smelly hands. The DC got the most private part of the hut, which meant he was somewhat spared the smells emanating from his unwashed non-vegetarian colleagues.

The next morning we were woken early, as we wanted to hit the trail before the sun rose too high. After an hour or so, we halted at a village for the morning meal which was more of the same: sticky rice and pork or chicken. As we walked into the village, smaller than the one we had left, we passed the only solid structure there – the shiny new little church. We could hear the morning service in progress, and slowing down at the DC's signal, stopped outside to hear the rest of the sermon. In rich and unmistakable Malayalam accent, the priest was haranguing his audience that had obviously annoyed him in some way. Their transgression had provoked him to utter horrific threats and he warned them that more of the same acts of omission would invite terrible retribution from the heavens. The DC listened for a while, then spoke briefly with the SDO. When he turned back to wait for the sermon to end, his mouth was set in a thin line, which meant he was not in a pleasant mood.

His expression openly defiant and almost arrogant, the priest walked out to where we waited. The power wielded by parish priests in the hill areas was well known and accepted as a fact of life by both officers of the district administration as well as the politicians who, instead of trying to counter this power, bent their minds to ways of using it to their advantage. This priest was not impressed by the presence of the DC, and he showed it through his stride. He was a lean, small-built chap, with a shock of curly hair that was well oiled in the manner of many Kerala men. He also sported a trimmed beard and was attired in tight-fitting trousers and a full-sleeved shirt buttoned at the wrists. He extended his hand in greeting, saying, 'Welcome! I am Father Joseph, the parish priest.'

The DC looked down at the hand and deliberately taking his time, extended his own, and while they shook hands, responded, 'And I am the deputy commissioner. You are new here, because when I was here last, Father Paul was parish priest.'

The man of God sensed the edge in the DC's polite words but continued to act relaxed. He looked around at the others, a cocky smile on his face, trying to include them in the exchange.

The DC continued, 'I present CB the probationer, and that is John the Baptist.'

The priest's face paled and a flush suffused his countenance. Hot words bubbled up to his lips, whose utterance was prevented by the timely intervention of my colleague John who, speaking in Malayalam, clarified that his name was John indeed, and that he was actually a Baptist. Somewhat mollified, but still smarting, the priest now found himself being taken by the arm by the DC and led away from the others.

The pleasant expression vanished from the DC's face as he spoke. 'The SDO told me why you are annoyed with the villagers, leading you to threaten them with all sorts of terrible things. What happens inside the church is your business, my friend, but these people are my responsibility too. And I take my responsibilities seriously. They are simple, trusting, God-fearing people who can be easy prey to unscrupulous outsiders. It is part of my job to see this is not allowed to happen. It is up to them to willingly give anyone any kind of gift. But I will not tolerate coercion of any kind. If I hear that you have misused your religious authority to extract offerings of any kind from the villagers again, I will return, and you will not find that a pleasant meeting. And do not try to seek shelter behind the plea of religious freedom. Have I made myself clear, my friend? If you have any doubts, I suggest you ask your predecessor about me. For your sake, I hope we will not have to discuss this subject again.'

With a pat on the back of the by now thoroughly chastened parish priest, the DC walked back to where the others stood. The ones who had left to finish their little private business behind the bushes had rejoined the group as well. The group proceeded on its way to the headman's hut, no one the wiser about what had transpired between the DC and the parish priest.

In this way was born the little legend of the visit of John the Baptist to the remote little village in Tamenglong District. The real John was a good friend, both of us natives of Kollam, Kerala. In fact, our connection appeared to go back even before that, to the time when midwife Joshua (John's grandmother) officiated at my birth in my grandparents' home in Kollam. And it was in Kollam that I saw John again for the last time, at the funeral service held in his memory. John was killed in a tragic mishap on the Dimapur–Kaziranga highway, when a truck collided headlong with the jeep in which he was travelling with the same DC who is featured in this piece. The latter survived, although he had to undergo a long and painful period of treatment and recovery before he could return to work.

I was invited by the parish priest of the church at Kollam to say a few words about John. In the front row I could see John's mother as she sat erect and dry-eyed, consoling others seated with her. As everybody waited for me to speak, his dark face with the curly hair and smiling mouth rose before my eyes and my thoughts went back to the first time I met John in Mussoorie, to other meetings with him there, to our journey together to Manipur and some funny incidents there. I started to get animated as I described this Peter Pan–like guy who approached everything he did with a certain innocence, youthfulness and freshness. Many in the till-then silent church began to smile and even laugh, remembering the cheerful young man who had been the life and soul of every gathering he attended, and whose untimely demise had left a large hole, difficult to fill.

Flag Hoisting at the DC's Bungalow

One of the drawbacks of studying at a boarding school is that one is condemned to rising at the crack of dawn for the rest of one's life, even on Sundays and other holidays. Having been hauled out of bed at an ungodly hour from the age of six to the sound of a braying bugle, and stumbling sleepily around trying to brush my teeth, while looking for a matching pair of socks to wear with the running shoes, and hopping along, accomplishing the difficult feat of slipping into a pair of shorts on the run, it is difficult in later life to lie in bed in silent contemplation of the day stretching ahead of oneself. While I didn't exactly spring out of bed with a cry of happiness each morning, I always found myself sitting, head in hands, wondering why I was up when the watch showed 5 a.m.! It did not help that the sun was shining brightly at that time, Indian Standard Time being at least an hour behind the sun in Manipur.

After a minute or two of gloomy contemplation of these longitudinal realities and their implications, my face would clear as the warmth of the day seeped through the cold walls of the bungalow. Rising, I would quickly complete my morning ablutions. The morning cuppa would have to wait since the orderly would still be deep in slumber. The other option was to walk over to the DC's bungalow across the road.

One day, deciding that a hot cup of tea was what I needed, I pulled on my walking shoes and walked out into the sunny but cold morning air. Swinging my arms about in what I imagined was a gymnastic loosening up routine, I crossed the road and entered the DC's bungalow compound.

This was a large tract, occupying the crest of a small hill overlooking the rest of the town, and it was dominated by the bungalow that was built on five-foot stilts. This left a space under the bungalow that became home to an assortment of the flora and fauna of the region. The luxuriant vegetation had defeated the efforts of the staff to keep this nether region clean and shrub free, and one could only speculate about the dangers that lurked within. Domingo was known to start from deep slumber and bark at the floorboards – at some unseen foe lurking below – while on occasion, the cat's fur would rise and stand on end, she having probably heard the slither of a snake underneath. Or the DC himself would be roused from sleep by a titanic battle under the floorboards between small armies, rending the silence of the night with their yelps and snarls and howls and hisses.

The bungalow itself was modelled on the tea garden bungalows of Upper Assam, with a wide veranda running all round the house. The deep-set walls had wide windows and doors, leading into tastefully decorated spacious rooms. I did not have eyes at that time of the day for the aesthetic accomplishments of the DC, but was intent on locating the cook in order to get a cup of hot tea. Finding the Nepali cook already brewing a pot of tea, I returned to the drawing room to wait. On sensing my presence, Domingo barked from the bedroom that he shared with the DC, which probably woke up the DC, for I could hear the soft slap of slipper-clad feet on the wooden floor. The door to the bedroom opened and the large form of Domingo bounded out to examine me, and after a few sniffs reassured him that I was non-threatening, he shambled off down the steps to the far end of the garden.

The cook appeared with a tray and two steaming cups of tea, which he placed on the table. The previous day's newspaper – which would have arrived the previous evening from Imphal – lay neatly folded alongside. The DC appeared in his dressing gown, loose pyjama bottoms dragging on the floor. I stood up and greeted him, which he answered with a smile. Seating himself in his easy chair, he opened the newspaper and, sipping his tea, enquired about my colleague who had not yet risen from his slumber. Silence fell while he absorbed himself in the contents of the day-old newspaper, reading about things that had happened two days ago in a world that appeared suddenly very remote. I reached over and picked up a several-weeks-old copy of the *Illustrated Weekly of India* and desultorily leafed through the contents before going through the comic strip section that I had never missed since early childhood. The minutes passed in this fashion, till the silence was broken by the loud barking of Domingo. The DC rose to take a look and, returning after a few minutes, invited me to join him out on the veranda.

The front of the house faced a large, square open space, bordered by flower beds. Beyond the square, the ground rose on all sides, creating an amphitheatre-like arena, where the only drama was when an enraged Domingo chased a particularly annoying cat across the ground and up a tree, or when a foraging squirrel was ambushed by a stalking cat, or when a mouse was caught in the claws of a swooping owl. These small tragedies (and victories) played themselves out unnoticed by the humans sharing the same compound. On one side of the square, the ground sloped up a little way and then flattened out for a short distance where a flagpole stood, before rising again, only to fall away steeply on the far side to the Central Reserve Police Force (CRPF) camp below. The DC narrated with ill-concealed glee his attempts to bombard the camp with 'rockets' and other firecrackers during the previous Diwali. Naturally, the soldiers could not retaliate, and must have seethed in impotent rage while the brilliantly coloured rockets rained down with impunity from the DC's compound.

I sat in one of the cane chairs arranged around a low table and looked out over the morning landscape. I found we were at one of the highest points in the valley housing the town of Tamenglong, the headquarters of West District. In order to see the rest of the town, I would have to walk over to the top of the knolls that framed the lawn. It was not yet six in the morning, but the sun appeared to be quite high and the birdsong had started to get muted as the foraging birds slowly departed for shelter from the sun that could be quite sharp even in winter. The DC appeared lost in thought as he gazed out at the mountains that seemed to rise like waves into the far distance. In that part of Manipur, the mountain ranges run parallel, separated by deep valleys cut by swift rivers. This made communication difficult. Roads were scarce, with most touring having to be done on foot. And as we found during the tours we went on with the DC, the villages were spaced a day's march apart.

Leaving the DC with his thoughts, I strolled out into the lawn, mug in one hand, a lighted cigarette in the other. I walked past the flagpole and climbed the little knoll. From there, I could get an excellent view of the CRPF encampment, and beyond at the town, which consisted of little more than a collection of houses strewn untidily in the valley, joined by irregular brown lines, presumably roads. Smoke rose in steady pillars from cooking fires, and morning sounds of human habitation had replaced the sounds of nature. However, one noise that was ever present in any urban habitation was completely and noticeably absent – the hum of vehicles. Once in a while, a jeep would roar out of the CRPF camp, or a scooter tear the morning silence with its typical tin-roof-rending growl. Less frequently, a heavily laden truck would groan up the road. Sound carries long distances in the hills. As children, my brother and I could pinpoint the position of every vehicle as it negotiated every curve and slope and hairpin bend near our house in the plantations.

The smells of cooking wafting up from the CRPF camp reminded me that I was hungry too. I was just about to begin wondering when breakfast would be ready when I heard the DC call me. Gulping down the last of my tea, I hurried down and found him standing near the flagpole. One of the Nepali boys working in the house hurried up with a bundle under his arm, which I saw was a faded tricolour. The DC smiled and said, 'You will now witness a much-loved ritual of the frontier areas: the hoisting of the tricolour in the morning. The flag represents the awesome majesty of Government with a capital G, and will flutter splendidly all day, come rain or sunshine, till it is lowered at sunset, only to be hoisted again the next day, and so it will measure the days as they flow, one into the next.'

This was an unusually long speech by the DC's standards, and very warm and almost emotional. My surprise must have shown, for the DC grinned and gestured to me to look at the lawn. There, marching towards us was Domingo, followed by the cat, then a duck and a rooster. Bringing up the rear was a goat. The ragged line halted and waited patiently when Domingo abruptly stopped to get over a veritable frenzy of scratching. Once he resumed his sedate walk, the troop followed and, as we watched in fascination, the creatures wheeled around and stood facing the flagpole. Now the parade was apparently called to order and we waited expectantly for the next manoeuvre.

It was then that I discovered that the Nepali with the flag had vanished. The DC, guessing the reason for my perplexity, gestured with his head upwards, and there, to my utter astonishment, I saw the lad shinnying up the pole like the toddy tappers of Kerala, with effortless and gravity-defying ease. As I watched transfixed, the lambu set about the task of fixing the flag to the pole. There appeared to be two tiny metal hooks fixed on the pole and he concentrated on the task of tying the flag to these hooks. It was obviously not an easy task, especially with one's legs wrapped round a slippery slender flagpole perched about a dozen feet off the ground. He completed the task, watched solemnly by the DC and me, as well as the formation led by Domingo. As he started to shimmy down, the DC's sharp voice brought him up short.

'Ji shaab?' he enquired.

'Bahadur, I'm afraid you will have to do it all over again.'

The boy looked puzzled and examined his handiwork again, and found the knots secure. As he started to come down, he was again arrested by the DC's dry, patient voice. 'The flag is upside down, my friend,' he said genially. The lad climbed back up and peered at the flag, which looked perfectly fine to him. Finally, through a combination of gestures and mime, the message was conveyed, and he gave us a huge smile as he retied the flag, correct side up. This time he looked down uncertainly and, sporting a wide smile on getting a nod from the DC, shimmied down, landing with a thud. He backed off a couple of paces and, in what can only be described as an attempt to lampoon the military, jerkily goose-stepped backwards, coming to attention with a thumping of both feet, and his arm flashed sideways and across in marionette-like movements till he completed what was easily the most impressive salute I have ever witnessed, his open hand vibrating like a tuning fork. It took a great effort not to break out laughing, and I could see that the DC, despite seeing this exhibition every morning, had not tired of it either. Domingo and troop impassively looked on, not having broken ranks yet. When the youngster finally lowered his arm, the DC thanked him formally and turned to return to the shade of the veranda. I waited to see what the rest of the parade would do, and saw Domingo turn to give an enquiring look to one of the troop. Someone, possibly the duck, appeared to say something, and the troop dispersed in an orderly fashion, going off in different directions.

We returned to the cane chairs, and the DC continued with his reading as if he had just participated in a normal flag-hoisting ceremony of the kind carried out daily in a hundred other locations in the country. I sat silent, my head full of the surreal tableaux I had witnessed. Finally, more out of a desire to start a conversation than anything else, I asked, 'That's a fine cat you have, sir. What do you call her?'

'Billi,' came the dry response. 'And the duck is called Batak, and the goat, Bakra. The rooster doesn't speak Hindi, and answers to Kozhi!'

Silence reigned once again as I digested this information. I could see the tricolour fluttering and snapping in the brisk wind that had started to blow. The lawn was deserted and quiet. Another day had started in Tamenglong.

Contempt of Court

I had been with the DC, Tamenglong, for over a week as part of the DC's office attachment, as was described in the cyclostyled, barely legible document from the undersecretary, Department of Personnel. There were two of us, and we were billeted in the inspection bungalow adjacent to the DC's. While hardly luxurious, the accommodation was comfortable. The lights came on at six every evening when the generator supplying power to the town was switched on. Since the lights went out at 10.30 in the night, we learnt to go to sleep early, while the fans (or heaters, depending on the season) still worked.

I did not like to lie in bed after daybreak, and with a mug of hot tea, would sit out on the veranda, watching the morning sun gradually change from ochre to brilliant gold, and the mountains from a dark featureless mass to lines of serrated ranges in various shades of green. My colleague, however, enjoyed his sleep, and seemed unworried about losing a few minutes of daylight as long as he could snore undisturbed.

One day, feeling more energetic than usual, I pulled on my track pants and a T-shirt and began jogging down the road, till a chorus of barks indicated that the dogs of the locality had decided to join me in the morning exercise, whereupon I slowed to a walk, having a healthy regard for the local canines after hearing the DC's blood-curdling (and no doubt exaggerated) accounts of their ferocity. The pack trotted up and looked at me, tails furiously brushing up a storm of dust, inviting me to resume my jogging so that they could join too. I, however, resolutely continued my walk to the disgust of the spirited pack, which expressed its disapproval with derisive barks and ironic coyote howls.

Tamenglong was located on a valley about 3,000 ft above sea level and it was therefore quite chilly in the early morning even in summer. The sun was high in the sky despite it being only 6 a.m. It was warm and pleasant as long as one remained in the sun, but if a cloud passed over it, or if one found oneself in a patch of shade, it turned cool in a trice. So the trick was to stay clear of the sides of the roads, and hope that there were no clouds about. As I resumed my jogging, having turned a curve and being lost to the sight of the canine gang, I looked around me to drink in the morning colours. The dominant note was green, in more shades than I imagined existed. No two trees in the forest appeared to have exactly the same colour, and every shade of green – from the deepest amethyst and emerald and jade to delicate pastels – stretched as far as the eye could see. The calling of birds, as they swooped about in pairs, filled the air with a symphony of sound, mostly in the higher octaves, with the occasional deeper call of the crow pheasant to provide a contrast. An hour later, having jogged and walked for quite a distance towards the Naga village on the far side of the little town, I was on my way back and passing by the CRPF encampment that stood between the DC's bungalow and the town.

I could hear the morning drills being conducted with orders barked and boots thudding on the well-rolled parade ground. I slowed to a walk and watched the troops march and wheel about in formation, a sight that never ceased to hold my attention ever since childhood. I walked on and turned into the large compound that housed the police wireless station with its tall mast, the DC's bungalow, and the inspection bungalow.

As I passed the wireless station, I heard the dry voice of the DC, who was engaged in a wireless conversation with someone.

Seeing me, he beckoned me, all the while continuing to speak into the mike. He gestured to the constable sitting behind the set, and the latter turned up the volume so that I too could hear the words of the speaker at the other end: 'As I have explained, RN, I have a report from the deputy inspector general (DIG) that a serious situation is developing in Tamenglong town. I would therefore like you to impose Section 144 and dusk-to-dawn curfew in the town limits. Over.'

The DC replied, 'I have studied the situation and am monitoring it hourly. It is true there was a fracas between some local youth and a couple of Bihari shopkeepers. There is no trouble now, and we are keeping a watch on the likely troublemakers. I see no need to impose prohibitory orders at this stage.'

'The DIG's report is quite categorical,' the disembodied voice crackled with ill-concealed irritation. 'Anyway, I would like you to do as I instruct. Is that clear?'

'I'm sorry, sir. I don't think I will be able to do as you instruct. As I mentioned, I do not see any reason to impose prohibitory orders at this point.'

'You will do exactly as told, RN,' barked the wireless set. 'This is a direct order.'

The DC looked at me with a grin that did not, however, reach his eyes, which were narrowed in concentration. He spoke: 'I'm afraid such an order will not be in order, sir. Therefore I regret I cannot obey such an order.'

'What the devil are you drivelling about?' shouted the other, clearly losing his temper. 'This is the chief secretary (CS) speaking, and I am giving you a direct order. Is that understood?'

The DC grinned more broadly and winked at me as he cleared his throat and spoke: 'I am acting in my capacity as DM when I consider the law and order situation. I have to satisfy myself that there is an imminent threat to public peace and tranquillity. I do not see such a situation existing at present. So I cannot issue the orders you want me to issue.'

The voice at the other end had become apoplectic and rose to a high-pitched shout: 'You will be in serious trouble, RN, unless you tell me that you will act as instructed. I will suspend you, and will ...' The voice trailed off in a staccato burst of static, while the DC calmly waited, regarding me with a half smile. I stood there nervously, wondering whether the man had lost his senses, and fearing that I too would get sucked into this brawl simply because I happened to be standing at the scene of action.

The wireless set was silent, save for the faint hum in the background that most electronic equipment used to emit. Finally, after what seemed to me a very long time, it crackled to life again: 'I hope to hear that you have reconsidered and will do as I instructed.'

The DC looked thoughtful. He raised an eyebrow at me interrogatively, as if asking my opinion on what he should do. I studiously looked away and saw him grin at my discomfiture. He cleared his throat and replied, 'I'm sorry, sir. But I cannot do as you wish. I would also like to point out that any attempt to interfere with my work in my capacity as DM would possibly amount to contempt of court!' He grinned as he said this, although there was no laughter in his voice, and waited for the response. The set remained silent, except for a crackle or two. The seconds stretched into minutes, and it was only after about five minutes that we realized that the CS had probably hung up at the other end.

The DC rose, stretched, and as he was leaving, signalled me to follow, then strode across the ground separating us from his bungalow, blithely unmindful of the storm that must be raging in Imphal. We sat down to steaming cups of tea and I ventured to speak for the first time since the verbal duel I had been made unwilling witness to. 'Will you not get into trouble over this, RN?' I asked. He held his cup in both hands and sipped noisily before replying, 'Well, I could have heard him out and then done exactly what I thought right. But I don't like the fellow, and this is not the first time I have had a run-in with him. And it's not going to be the last time either. Of course he will be furious. Of course there will be consequences. I will probably be transferred. That is a risk one runs. The way I see it, in a place like Manipur, one has every reason to be honest and correct. You are anyway thousands of miles from home. If you are transferred, you are going to be only a few miles farther from home. They cannot transfer me to Burma, can they? So, what the hell!'

He went on to narrate a similar episode that had happened when he was DC at Ukhrul, or what was East District in those days. It was more or less on the same lines, with only the CS being a different person, and this time involving an army officer who was a close friend of the CS. This officer had a roving eye, and a weakness for young local girls. He was a smart fellow and cut a dashing figure in his uniform. He had an air of being a man of the world, which must have made him attractive to young women. One such liaison had been going on for a few weeks, but matters came to a head when the brother of the girl involved protested hotly when the jeep came to fetch the young woman. The jeep returned without the girl, and this apparently infuriated the waiting officer. He dispatched a posse of soldiers, who tracked down the brother and gave the young man a sound thrashing. Hearing of this, the villagers squatted on the highway, preventing traffic from moving. The DC had to intervene to defuse the situation.

However, the army officer was not content to let the matter die down. He sent an alarming report suggesting there was insurgent activity in that village, requiring an immediate search of houses. He requested the state administration to pass prohibitory orders to facilitate the army in its task. A signal was sent to the DC to act, and RN, who was the DC there, refused saying that conditions did not warrant such an extreme step. The officer stood by his report, and the CS supported him, but the DC would not relent. The CS suspended the DC and transferred him, pending enquiry. What happened next was typical of the north-east. Villagers climbed on to trucks and assorted vehicles and travelled to Imphal, where they barged into the CM's house. The CM at the time was from Ukhrul. They staged a sit-in at his house till the transfer orders were withdrawn, and returned to their village after helping themselves to a hearty lunch from the CM's kitchen! The DC was only too aware that the thwarted CS would find other ways of getting back at him, and so managed to persuade the villagers that the transfer was in order, but was a routine transfer rather than a punishment. He later heard that his successor did as the CS instructed. Curfew was imposed and the whole village was punished for what the army officer saw as the insolence of a young man trying to protect his sister.

The sordid story had an unfortunate sequel, which I heard later from another source. The episode was reported in the press, and the army ordered an enquiry. The officer involved probably realized that he would be in trouble. So he contrived to frame a younger officer from his own unit, arranging for the unfortunate chap to be found in an inebriated condition with the girl in question. The young officer was found guilty of the charges and sent on a punishment transfer to another distant army post in a far corner of the country.

Domingo let out a rumbling sound that was the nearest I had heard a dog come to purring as the DC scratched him behind his floppy ear. My watch showed that it was not yet half past seven in the morning. Another day had begun. I wondered how it would end, as the inevitable consequences of the exchange I had been witness to a few minutes earlier would begin to flow.

The Courtesy Call

I could see the sun-drenched street from where I sat – back to the wall, behind a large table, a few chairs in the two rows in front. Cupboards and shelves with files lined the walls; the far wall was bare, save for a picture of Gandhi with his toothless grin and a calendar, obviously government-issued, with holidays boldly marked in red. *This is obviously the local holiday season*, I thought, cheering up as I spotted several red cells.

My first day on the job had not begun well. I was at the office ten minutes ahead of time and had to wait for a further thirty minutes while someone went hurrying off to find the fellow who had the keys. Pacing up and down the veranda in full view of the passers-by, my irritation grew as the minutes ticked. When the worthy eventually bustled up and began fumbling with the keys, even I could see the humour in the situation and joined the small crowd that had gathered and began giving helpful suggestions on how to get the door open. When it was finally unlocked, I saw many of the bystanders troop in after me. They were obviously members of the staff of my new office and went to their desks giving me curious but not unfriendly looks.

The first few minutes went swiftly, with a curious ritual resembling a roll call in a school being enacted as each person stood up with an abashed expression when the names were called, and mumbled something unintelligible about the work he or she did. Most men were smartly turned out in well-cut coats and matched ties, the women pretty in their long sarongs wound tight around their hips. Most of them spoke good English; so that was one mountain less to climb, I thought.

I pulled out a slip of paper from my coat pocket – the checklist of things to do on my first day that I had prepared diligently. The first item was 'Speak to office staff', where I intended to say how happy I was to be in the office, how lovely the place was, how much I had heard of their diligence and friendliness, and that I looked forward to their full cooperation. But things had not gone according to plan so far and I dropped the idea of the speech. Having decided to skip this item, I went to the next one – to have a discussion with the office superintendent regarding the workflow, the way work was assigned, and pending issues.

The urbane, smiling man who came in and sat in front of me obviously had little idea of what I was saying, and smiled more broadly when I finished and waited for him to speak. The silence and smiles grew longer. He fiddled with his tie, his pen, the papers in front of him, as I searched for something to say. Finally, inspiration struck and I said: 'Thank you.' With vast dignity he rose and, inclining his head courteously, left the room with the air of a man who had done his best to be helpful. I stared at the empty chairs in front, wondering about my next move. My eyes fell on the checklist still open before me on the desk and, with a sigh, moved to the next item.

There was a soft cough and I looked up to see a dapper man. I invited him to sit and waited expectantly for him to state his business. He smiled back with a helpful expression and I realized that he was waiting for me to speak.

'I am new here and this is my first day in office. Is there anything I can do for you?' I said, radiating cooperation and, I hoped, competence.

'Pleased to meet you, sir,' he replied, extending his hand which I took. 'I am Peter, SDO, Ukhrul,' he continued.

I started violently, as if a thousand volts had passed through my hand. Was this some kind of practical joke? He continued to pump my hand enthusiastically. Searching desperately for something to say, I stammered, 'That's odd, because I am the SDO, Ukhrul.'

He smiled tolerantly. Then, with a deprecating wave of his hand, hastened to reassure me: 'I'm with the Revolutionary Government of Manipur.'

My hand still in his, I thought wildly that I was imagining the whole thing. The RGM was the acronym for the underground movement that was fighting a low-intensity guerrilla campaign against the government. With nothing to say, I had little option but to continue to let my hand be shaken, trying at the same time to extricate it from the man's grip. He looked happy, with the air of a man who had got through the difficult but necessary task of introductions, and appeared ready and willing to move to the next stage in the proceedings.

Should I offer him a cup of tea? Why not, and anyway I don't know how to handle the situation. At least not yet. Is he really a member of the underground? He looks a decent sort of chap, quite normal in appearance. He could have been a schoolteacher, or a clerk, or a shop assistant. But a terrorist? Are all members of underground movements 'terrorists'? The semantic aspects of this issue appeared a promising line of thought, but then another thought intruded: *What should a terrorist look like? With a Zapata moustache and bandoliers of ammunition strung across his chest?* Had I seen any pictures of terrorists or members of the underground? What did they look like? I realized I must have glanced over hundreds of pictures of guerrilla fighters and terrorists, dead and alive, in *TIME* and *LIFE*, but couldn't recollect what their faces looked like!

My opposite number (I had already started to think of him as a functionary or official!) was happy to accept the offer of tea, which we sipped in congenial silence as I searched for something to say. He prattled on about the good points of the district and offered helpful tips on where to go and what to see. The chap was actually being quite nice and there I was, wondering about what terrorists looked like. *Should I be sitting here talking to a self-proclaimed member of the underground? Am I not supposed to call for the police to arrest him and clap him in irons? To make him rot in jail so that the constitutional government could go about its work and the free citizens of Ukhrul about theirs? Is my behaviour not treasonous, inviting dire consequences the least of which would be dismissal from service?* These and other thoughts bubbled and frothed in the cauldron that my mind had become, as I tried vainly to follow his tips on how to make the best of my tenure in Ukhrul.

With some effort, I brought myself back to the present and tried to listen to what he was saying. 'And of course you have a fine view of the state flower of Manipur, the Siroy lily that blooms on the slopes of the Siroy mountain that looms across the valley from your quarters. This lovely blossom blankets the slopes of the mountain and makes it appear pinkish white. You will have to wait till spring to see it bloom, but I assure you it is a sight worth waiting for.' He had a faraway look and stared out of the window, at a distant vision of the famed flower, perhaps remembering picking a few blossoms for the girl he loved.

'We Tangkhuls are an interesting lot, and too clever by half. We're always quarrelling and appear to have an inexhaustible store of issues over which to fight. On a more serious note, Tangkhul youth have taken to education faster than any of the other hill tribes, and as a result, many of our people have made it to the IAS and higher services. Our young people study in the best universities in India and go on to seek careers in varied fields. We are part of the Naga nation, but the other major Naga tribes like the Ao and Angami fear and respect us. Although there has been a demand for a greater Nagaland, comprising the contiguous Naga areas of states like Manipur, Assam and Arunachal Pradesh, I don't believe the Ao and Angami are very enthusiastic about following up on that demand since that will bring the Tangkhuls into the political calculus. Muivah (one of the key leaders of the

Naga underground) is a Tangkhul, as are many other top commanders of the Naga underground. I myself am from Tolloi, which you can see on that ridge,' he concluded.

The door to the inner office opened and the urbane superintendent entered, crossed the room, extracted a file from the cupboard, and with a murmured greeting to the man seated across me, vanished through the door. Did he not recognize this man? Had the entire SDO office been infiltrated? My thoughts were interrupted when the man opposite me stood up and regretfully informed me that he had work to do and looked forward to meeting me more often in future. I followed his figure down the dusty road till he turned into a lane and vanished from sight.

No sooner had he left than I pressed the buzzer to summon the superintendent and demand an explanation for what was going on. He seemed quite unperturbed and explained, as if to a child, that there was a parallel government structure of the underground elements, replicating faithfully the official superstructure to the minutest detail. *So they must also be overstaffed and inefficient and slothful*, I thought unkindly, imagining the forests crowded with underemployed clerks and other office staff of the underground government roaming around with little to do. *God, the bloody forests must be alive with these chaps. It's a wonder the security forces don't stumble across more of them during their patrols. They must easily outnumber their fighting comrades*, I thought. Surely, the best way to counter them would be to allow them to collapse under the deadweight of their own bureaucracy!

The rest of the day went by in a mind-numbing succession of introductions and 'courtesy calls', with a procession of officials of all descriptions dropping in to say 'hello' to the new arrival. I was staggered at the number of officials even in this little hill town tucked away in a remote corner of the country. With their pronounced Indo-Chinese features, they all looked the same to my plainsman's eye, and I began to wonder whether this was a trick, with the same set of people walking out through one door, only to enter through another claiming to be so-and-so from such-and-such department. Each one was either a deputy so-and-so or assistant so-and-so or additional so-and-so or joint so-and-so or chief so-and-so. The acronyms for various obscure departments and organizations flew fast and furious, with IHADP elbowing aside ICDS which squeezed ahead of NREP which trampled upon SFDA.

In the evening, peace descended on the office, with the staff members briskly winding up their affairs and sitting ready for departure before closing time. I sat at my desk, the now silent office allowing sounds from the street to filter in: a dog barking nearby, children laughing and chasing each other through the dusty street, a bus or truck groaning up an unseen slope, a church bell sending peals rolling down the wooded hillsides. Daylight started to fade, and as the darkness gathered, the silence too grew, till the ticking of the elderly clock on the far wall sounded like castanets playing at a slow tempo. It was only five-thirty in the evening, but already dark. I realized we were far to the east, where Indian Standard Time didn't make much sense; where the sun rose at five in the morning and jeeps had to put on their headlamps at four in the afternoon.

I realized that I should be making my way back to the quarters at the far end of the town. The generator that supplied power to it would soon be cranked on and the lights would first flicker and then settle to a steady glow as the generator got into top gear. Another day had drawn to a close in the little hill town of Ukhrul, and as I sat in the jeep that was bumping its way through the road leading to my quarters, my first day on the job as an IAS officer on my first posting too started to wind down. Passing by the Police Recreation Club, I could see a pair playing table tennis, watched by a group of youngsters. I resolved to go over the next day after office and try my hand at a game, something I had not done in a long time. I had already forgotten my encounter with my counterpart from the underground, a fact that later I found to be remarkable, considering that I was new to the area and the job. Perhaps this was just the way the place got to you, making the most unusual things look ordinary. I could see that I was in for an interesting time. I pulled my coat tighter about me as the jeep rattled its noisy way through the winding lanes.

The War and Peace of
Father Mathew and Father John

It was already dark as the jeep turned into the gate. I climbed out, clutching some files bound in red tape and string, and looked on as the driver hauled out a case of files from the rear seat and manhandled it up the steps into the house. The house was dark, the generator powering the lights of the town not having been switched on. Along the ridge, tiny lights, probably gas lanterns, winked in the darkness as Ukhrul settled down to another night.

In the faint moonlight cast by a sliver of a moon, the bulk of the Siroy mountain loomed in front. Three vehicles climbing the road that cut a steady line across the slope of the mountain could be seen on their way to Jessami further to the north. As I stood taking in the scene, the lights in the house flickered on, dimmed and flared alternately for a while, and then settled to a steady glare. To an outsider they created the illusion of a boat on a dark sea at night, as the nearest house was quite a distance away, hidden behind trees. The brilliant starlit sky spanned my vision in every direction till it met the inky darkness of the ground. I had never seen the stars shine so brightly; I almost felt I could see my shadow by starlight!

I started at the voice at my shoulder, one of the lambus having spoken. He spoke only Naga and Assamese, but I found little difficulty in communicating with him using a combination of mime, broken English and broken Hindi. He was obviously calling me to come into the house as it was getting chilly, with a sharp wind blowing. With the door shut firmly behind me, I felt warmer, although one could still hear the wind howl outside. The 'Assam-type' construction – consisting of wooden frames and bamboo mat plastered with clay fastened onto the frame – was very effective in keeping the wind and water out although, together with the corrugated tin roof, it did not succeed in keeping out the sounds of the night. When it rained and the wind howled, one could hear every drop fall on the roof, every sigh of the wind, every clockwork stutter of each cricket in the vicinity and every phlegmatic croak of each passing bullfrog. Conversation on such occasions therefore had to be conducted at high decibels, which increased the theatricality of the scene of two people seated across a small table in a small room, shouting to make themselves heard over the din of nature's orchestra performing at full volume outside!

Despite the doors being closed, and the maifu (a coal-burning stove used to heat rooms) roaring away, emitting more sound and light than heat, the cold was beginning to get through to me. I decided against a hot bath and changing instead into a lungi and kurta and a thick cardigan, poured myself a large shot of rum, added hot water, and sat in front of the maifu, twiddling with the dials of the little radio-cum-tape-recorder or two-in-one as it was called. After unsuccessfully surfing the airwaves trying to raise BBC on shortwave, I decided instead to listen to a cassette of M.D. Ramanathan and sat back as the deep sepulchral voice gradually gained strength and poured over me like balm, probing the majestic range of Raga Darbari. Although the volume was low, it sounded unusually loud as the wind outside had suddenly died down and silence had fallen over the mountainside. The warm rum burned its way down my throat with its bitter-sweet caramel taste spreading warmth through my insides. I took another sip and sat back thinking about the day that was just coming to a close. So many things had happened on my first day on the job that all I could do was smile wryly as I remembered some of them. There was enough time to think seriously about the implications of some of the experiences of the day and I was content to let my mind drift over the incidents.

I was roused from this reverie by the sound of a vehicle labouring up the road past the house, and I listened to the gears shifting and the pitch of the engine changing as it negotiated the steep slope just outside the gate. The sounds died, which could only mean that I had a visitor. Cursing under my breath since I was not dressed to receive visitors, I quickly pulled on a pair of trousers and entered the living room to see a large man in some sort of colourful shirt standing at the door, giving instructions to someone outside. He turned on hearing me enter and, stretching out a hand, said, 'I am Father Mathew from the Baptist Mission at the other end of town. I heard you had taken charge today and thought I would drop in and say hello.'

We shook hands, and I thought it very civil of him to have taken the trouble to come out on a cold evening just to welcome me. He had an arresting personality. Obviously a Malayali (a fact I gathered from his unmistakable accent), he was a shade under six feet tall, burly, with hairy forearms and tufts of hair growing out of his ears. He was clean-shaven, with thick lips and shiny white teeth. He wore a green-and-yellow ktenge – the collarless half-sleeve shirts popular in East Africa – and excellent olive-green corduroy trousers. His feet were in expensive Timberland hiking boots, and I could see a pair of good-quality socks above their rich leather. An expensive looking watch adorned his thick wrist and he sported two gold rings on fleshy fingers. Overall, he radiated well-being and affluence. Seeing my examination, he smiled disarmingly and said, 'As you can see, I like the good things in life. I hope you don't mind if I smoke.' Then he pulled open a silver tube, producing a cigar which he proceeded to light. I followed suit, lighting a cigarette from my pack.

We exchanged notes about which part of Kerala we were from, discovered we had some common acquaintances and I found myself warming to this genial man who was unlike any Christian priest I had encountered. He was a mine of information about the district, its flora and fauna, its history, its contemporary political equations, the underground movement, rival church factions, the CM's faction among the Tangkhul and the opposing rival group supported by the famous underground leader who lived somewhere in Burma, and so on. He pulled a bottle of rum out of the bag he had with him and, shouting to the lambu to bring glasses and water, poured two large drinks which, after clinking glasses, we downed with enthusiasm before proceeding to refill.

Outside, the noise levels had begun to climb with the wind starting up again, soon to be joined by the rest of the orchestra as the rain began to hammer down on the metal roof. And so we did not hear the second vehicle draw up and stop outside the gate. It was only when there was a knock on the door that we realized we had another visitor. *Well, well,* I thought to myself, *when it rains in these parts, it certainly pours!* I opened the door to admit a rotund figure in coat and flannels, and heard Father Mathew's pleased exclamation behind me, indicating he knew the visitor. Turning after shutting the door, I shook hands with the new arrival who introduced himself. 'I'm Father John, from the Catholic Church just down the road from your house, next to the Mission Hospital that we run. I heard about you having taken charge as SDO and thought I'd call on you. But I see that Father Mathew has beaten me to it. Anyway, I shall join you in a drink.' Then, without much ado, he poured himself a drink. We raised our glasses and took a large gulp each and I sat back, deciding to let the evening take its own course.

This was getting interesting. While the two priests appeared outwardly cordial and friendly, I could sense an antagonism between them that did not appear guided by their denominational differences alone.

The rest of the evening was spent reminiscing about Kerala, especially its cuisine. Both appeared to be connoisseurs of various kinds of food, especially that of central Travancore. And so the evening wore on with the names of popular dishes from that part of Kerala rolling off tongues as they sat, their gaze on distant scenes of swaying coconut palms and women swaying along narrow bunds with precariously balanced loads on their heads, conjuring up visions of mirror-like backwaters, with lotus and 'African payal' floating motionlessly on the surface, beguiling the viewer into thinking it to be solid earth with vegetation, and a neat line of ducks in perfect formation crossing narrow stretches of water. Glasses were emptied and refilled as remembered snatches of folk songs began to emerge from rum-lubricated throats, with the two priests looking archly at each other as risqué lines compared the generous attributes of a certain buxom Thankamma and winsome Leelamma. One of the lambus, apparently unsurprised at the revelry of the men of God, produced a heaped plate of fried chicken, while Father Mathew opened a can of Swiss cheese which he proceeded to spread on crisp crackers that he fished out of the same bag.

It was inevitably Father John who brought the evening to a close, clucking with annoyance and rebuking Father Mathew for having made him stay so late. 'The Sisters will be waiting for me to have dinner,' he scolded as he crossly wrapped the woollen scarf around his neck while Father Mathew made a naughty remark about the Mother Superior of the mission. At this, Father John seemed to struggle to suppress a smile and look severe, then stumped off to his jeep with a shouted 'goodnight' that was snatched away by the strong wind.

Father Mathew looked enquiringly at me and brushing aside my weak protest, refilled our glasses. He recounted his experiences in Ukhrul and in the north-east in general, speaking of the challenges of being a man of God in these inaccessible places. He spoke of the rivalry between various denominations, of the strategies used by each to wean people away from the other, of the retaliation when the stratagem was discovered, of the attitude of the Church higher-ups to these skirmishes. He spoke of the organization and methods of the Catholic Church with not a little admiration, and likened his ministry (he belonged to the Baptist Church) to a guerrilla operation in contrast. He explained why the strict rules and customs of the Catholics were the source of their strength in the face of adversity, and how it actually earned them the admiration and respect of the common man.

He stayed till very late, and as he left, he gave me a bear hug in the manner of an old friend. As his jeep disappeared slowly down the dark road, I returned to my chair, trying to digest the events of the evening. I must have dozed off in my chair, because when I woke, the sun was shining, and it was six in the morning!

Father John was more in the traditional mould, of conservative mien, serious about his mission, but making an effort to be seen as broad-minded, which had the effect of making him appear unctuous and condescending. Fiercely committed to the Roman Catholic Church, he would brook to opposition to its mission, and being a hard worker himself, he expected his team to give their best at all times. Severity was part of his make-up. While he was paternal towards his flock, and especially the priests and nuns in his team, he was unflinching in his dedication to his mission, to the point of appearing uncaring and unfeeling about the feelings of others. He felt answerable only to God, hence did not care what people thought of him. Truly a man of God, he thought politics was best left to the politicians.

In contrast Father Mathew's view of Christianity was that of a gentle and empowering faith, built by working among the poor and the needy, the weak and the powerless. This did not involve asceticism or severe personal deprivation or austerities of various kinds. Neither did it appear to be about strictly enforcing codes of conduct, warning people away from sin and inviting divine retribution down on those who ignored the advice. It was more about trying to understand people's problems and helping them make their lives better. He moved mostly among the ordinary people, spending little time inside his small unpretentious church, tramping up and down the muddy roads and sludge-filled fields, searching for more needy to reach. I could not help thinking how much more effective governance would be if we could attract a few people like Father Mathew.

The differences between the men ran deep and they knew it and did not attempt to hide the fact. Each believed what he did was a better way of serving God. But both being men who had seen the world in all its imperfections also knew when not to speak of these things.

During my brief sojourn at Ukhrul, I came to look forward to the arrival of these unusual men. Our weekly meetings were times when the two buried the hatchet and joined me in going on wondrous journeys down memory lane. Even today, images of the modest house resounding to priests singing ribald Malayalam ditties enumerating Thankamma's charms leave me smiling!

Postscript:

After my return from Manipur, I have been asked many times about the role of the Church in the affairs of the north-east. Most of these questions come loaded with suggestions about a dark agenda inimical to the Indian state being pursued by the Church. I have never been able to understand this insinuation. While the Church does wield some influence in Latin American countries and the Philippines, in my view, it has reconciled to a separation between the state and the Church.

The other insinuation is that religious minorities in India are somehow covertly anti-Indian. This too does not hold up to close scrutiny. I have attended church services in various parts of the country and have been moved by the priest invoking the blessing of the Almighty on the Indian nation, something I have never come across in any temple.

A few years ago, I learnt that Father Mathew was murdered in a remote village where he was tending his flock. I felt saddened at the news, knowing how well he loved the people he worked among and for. It appeared that he was killed by a member of one of the many splinter groups of the insurgent movement, probably because he spoke out against violence as a means to achieving any worthwhile end. There were many among the insurgents who frowned on Father Mathew's epicurean ways and probably thought that he was siphoning off funds meant for the poor. What they did not know was that most of the money he spent on the people was raised through his personal efforts, that the good things he appeared to have and enjoy were sent to him by loving siblings and family.

The day I heard the news, I raised a glass in his memory as my mind went back to chilly evenings spent with a warm man with a big heart.

The Nervous Breakdown

The morning sun slanted through the open windows as I stepped out into the small garden of the SDO's quarters. It was already bright and warm, although my watch showed it was still not yet 6 a.m. I wondered why the government did not think of a different time zone for the north-eastern region where the sun rose before 5 a.m. IST and set at around 4 p.m. in winter. It being Sunday, I was in my lungi–kurta with a warm cardigan to keep out the chill from the morning wind that sometimes blew. I was looking forward to a slow morning. I lit a cigarette and inhaling the smoke deeply, let it out in a long plume, watching it get caught in a gust of breeze and disintegrate into chaotic confetti.

The road in front of the gate disappeared over a rise some way after the compound fence to the west towards the town and to the east into a clump of trees. Across the road, the ground sloped away in a convex swell till it disappeared into the steep valley. Behind the house, the land dropped again, although less steeply, till it was met by the line of trees and the forest beyond. The road thus ran on a ridge along the spine of which was strung the little town of Ukhrul. It comprised a line of houses on either side of this road, with a few lanes where the slope permitted some more houses to perch on the available ground. One end was defined by the SDO's quarters, and the other by the Baptist Church. Actually, the eastern boundary was more accurately the Catholic Church and the Mission Hospital and Seminary further down the road from the SDO's house, beyond the clump of trees.

From where I stood, looking north, my gaze spanned the deep valley and the rising bulk of the Siroy mountain towering over the surrounding hills. The scar on the road blasted by the Border Roads Organisation (BRO) stood out like a fresh wound on the dense green forest that darkened as it vanished down the deep valley. Near the crest of the mountain was open grassland dotted with shrubs and a few trees on which the famed Siroy lily bloomed every seven years. That day, in the morning light, it looked more mauve than the brilliant blue for which it is justly famous.

A second cup of tea and the sports pages of the previous day's newspaper helped me pass the time as the morning wore lazily on. It almost felt like midday while sitting in the sun, although the mercury dropped when one moved into the shade. I knew that breakfast was still about an hour away, since Apang and Nelson, the lambus employed at the house, took that long to get together the breakfast of fried eggs, toast and coffee. The technique of parallel processing seemed to be too much for their sturdy minds and I had conceded defeat in trying to explain that it was quicker to get the toast done while the eggs were being fried, so that one got to eat both while hot and crisp.

The sound of a jeep drawing up brought me back to the present and, looking up from the newspaper, I saw someone get out of the vehicle, push open the gate, and walk up the path with hurried steps. It was an unfamiliar figure, and I got up slowly, wondering about the identity of the visitor and his purpose at the early hour on a Sunday morning.

Noting from his garb that he was probably an officer of some department, I invited him to take a seat on another chair placed on the lawn and offered him a cup of tea, which the other accepted with alacrity. I then waited for the other man to introduce himself, which he presently did, in a halting voice.

'I'm S.K. Singh, the IO here in Ukhrul.' Seeing my blank expression, he went on. 'I mean I'm the intelligence officer, from the Intelligence Bureau (IB).' I acknowledged this with a nod and waited for him to go on, which he did after appearing to collect his thoughts. 'I've been in Ukhrul for nearly two months now. I know that you have just come from Imphal on posting. So I thought I'd come over and say hello.' I thought it was very civil of him to have done so, and was in fact quite surprised since this was the first officer who had called at my house in the two weeks I had been there. That it should be an IO from the IB was a bit surprising.

The tea arrived and after a short pause while the brew was being poured and the mug handed over, he confided, 'This is my first posting in the north-east.' I thought wryly that it was my first posting too, but I did not say so immediately, so as not to lose whatever little advantage his disclosure may have given me. 'Interesting people, these Tangkhul Nagas,' Singh went on. 'Very friendly and hospitable. Also very intelligent. They probably contribute most of the leaders of the underground movement. The maximum number of Nagas inducted into the government services from the hills are from among the Tangkhuls. It is probably true that one factor dampening the demand for a greater Nagaland is that the Ao, Angami and other influential tribes of Nagaland are apprehensive of the Tangkhuls.' I knew that was correct since I had met a girl, also a Tangkhul, from the IAS batch immediately junior to mine, who was from Tolloi and who had two sisters in government service.

The conversation then proceeded to the happenings in Ukhrul, and mostly revolved around the activities of the underground. These appeared to be considerable, much more than reported in the press and far more commonplace than the officially accepted version at the officers' club common room. I noticed that the information being divulged was mostly of a general nature, probably common knowledge in these parts, and that nothing I had not already known or of real value had been imparted by the man.

Inwardly commending the other's caution in this respect, I asked about the incidence of schoolboys bunking school and joining the underground training camps across the border in Burma. Singh looked serious at this direct query and replied stiffly: 'I'm afraid you will have to ask the home department in Imphal.' Surprised at this response, I answered that all I wanted was an informal reply to this question which had an important bearing on the day-to-day work of the government machinery. Again, I was told that it was best I get the information through the proper channels.

Unwilling to let the matter pass unchallenged, I said, 'We are both officials, albeit in different arms of the government, posted in a little town barely a couple of hours as the crow flies from the Burma border. This is nearly 3,500 km from Delhi, and about the same distance from my home town. What you are saying is that if I want information on something that you have in your records, that information will have to flow from you to your higher-ups in Imphal, to the joint director (JD), IB, in Guwahati, to the IB in Delhi, to the home ministry in North Block, to the Government of Manipur or CS in Imphal, then to the home department, and thence through the deputy commissioner to me, the SDO here in Ukhrul?'

Singh's bald reply was: 'That's right.' He appeared pleased that I had understood the complexities involved so quickly. I looked to see whether there were more layers to his expression but I could read nothing more than a bland complacency. There was no trace of the humour I had hoped to find.

I went on heatedly: 'How the hell can we get anything done if this is the way the wheels of government grind? Of what bloody use is the information if it comes after a few months or weeks? The point about *knowing* that schoolboys are missing from school is to *do* something about it, to reassure worrying parents. After a few weeks, they are already across the border, with several doses of indoctrination injected into them.'

The response was rather placid. 'But the information has to be collated, validated, interpreted, analysed and presented in a form that can be of use. We can't just give raw, unverified information—'

'My dear chap, we don't want a bound copy of the report in triplicate. That may be necessary for the big shots in North Block, but we lowly guys do not need these things. What we *do* need is timely information about things affecting our work,' I interrupted.

I realized I was being unfair to Singh, who was doing a difficult and dangerous job in a remote corner of the country, far from his home. He was as bound by the rules and processes of his department as I was, and even if he did agree with me, he could do little to change the way things were done. And perhaps neither of us understood the issues involved fully, and therefore the processes and rules were probably needed, after all. But it was still quite frustrating.

Changing the subject, I spoke: 'You wanted to see me about something, but we seem to have got sidetracked.'

Singh looked embarrassed and appeared to be having second thoughts about what had brought him to my house in the first place. I continued to sip my tea. Finally, he appeared to reach a decision and, clearing his throat, ventured to speak. 'I got married recently, and in fact, soon after the wedding, was posted here. I was earlier posted at Meerut, fairly close to my home near Baghpat. My wife is from Roorkee and has spent all her life there. She is a qualified teacher, and was actually teaching at the local Kendriya Vidyalaya when we married. She knew about Manipur and actually looked forward to coming here, and so I hoped that we would be able to complete my posting here without any difficulty.'

He paused and appeared to be marshalling his thoughts. It was evident that he could go on only with some effort.

'But things have gone terribly wrong from the day we got to Ukhrul. My wife has not been able to settle down to the idea of being here for even a day, let alone for a couple of years. She cannot stand the thought of staying in the house when I am away at work, so much so that I am afraid to leave her alone at home. She does not sleep well, and has started to swallow sleeping pills at night. Her appetite has vanished and she finds it difficult to keep food down when she does eat. This has been going on for almost the entire two months we have been here, and I too am suffering from the strain of it all. I think my wife is near a total breakdown, and I am at my wits' end. There is no experienced doctor here to consult, and I am not sure whom I can trust even in Imphal. I know you have just come and that you are also in your first posting, but I had to talk to someone, or I thought I would go crazy.' He looked so miserable and confused that I wished I could say something to make him feel better.

I sympathized with Singh, and tried to imagine the days and nights he and his wife must have spent trying to grapple with their problem. Prisoners of their perceptions of the place and the people, they must have found the little society of the officer class in Ukhrul stiflingly tiny and closed. With little experience of and comfort with north-eastern mores, they would dismiss any possibility of developing friendships with the locals, making the problem worse.

In places that are quite alien to one, the sense of one's place in the scheme of things is severely tested, and one is often unable to stand the strain. I'm sure the husband and wife must have found the days passing slowly and the pressures growing, with no relief in sight. The few events in the social calendar must have served only to reinforce the couple's sense of alienation.

Mainlanders find themselves getting subtly separated into two distinct groups: those who succeed in getting a measure of acceptance into the local community and those who don't. Though it is true that blending into the new environs depends as much on one's willingness to mingle as on the other's wish to reciprocate.

In this respect, south Indians appeared to find it easier to make friends. It was interesting to speculate about the reasons why this should be so. Very few north Indians went to the south in search of jobs, and those who did usually formed their own groups that met for Holi and Diwali and spoke Hindi in an attempt to construct a familiar world for themselves. Perhaps, south Indians had greater experience of having to make a home far from their native place. They had to learn the language and adjust to the food and customs of the new place, and these skills therefore came much more easily to them.

I did not know what to tell the Singhs to help them out of their predicament, and judging from what the husband told me, the prognosis did not look good for the young couple. It would probably be for the best if they tried to get a transfer to some place like Guwahati. If that failed, perhaps the wife could return home and get her old job back, so that her self-worth was retained while they tried to figure out where to go from there.

It would not have been so bad if he had been in the army, where they would always be posted to a formation where they would live together and among their own kind, protected by the practices and rituals and customs of the army that must appear reassuring to all but the most independent minded. Here, he was posted to some far-flung outpost to serve alone among a strange people, doing a job that could be dangerous. Part of his job involved trying to fit in and merge with the local people, gaining their confidence so that he could gather the information and intelligence for which purpose he had been sent in the first place.

I guessed that many such little tragedies must have been enacted in these parts, and other similar places. In some cases, the families may have been successful in drawing back from the brink but in other cases, these efforts must have failed, with one or the other going off the edge, into the abyss of depression or even worse. An unknowing (and uncaring) bureaucracy probably dismissed these as the failure of young people to adjust to new places and realities, with smug senior officers shaking their heads and clucking about the younger generation not having enough of the right stuff.

I thought about my feelings at being posted to that distant and strange place, something that I had not bargained for when I took the UPSC exams. Then I found myself in a job that was part of a near-colonial administration, alienated from the local populace that was deeply resentful of our presence. There was something Kafkaesque about the situation, being an unwelcome stranger in a place not of my own choosing, doing a job involving policies that I did not wholly agree with, directed by and answerable to a distant authority I did not respect for its lack of knowledge of the realities on the ground.

I promised to drop in on them at the earliest opportunity and requested Singh to bring his wife home for dinner sometime soon. After he left, I had my misgivings about the idea of calling them over. I reflected on the usefulness of my efforts to introduce them to people like Father Mathew and Father John. Would those extraordinary men with the cross and cassock as well as the other colourful characters that populated my social life in Manipur be appreciated for who they truly were?

I poured myself a stiff glass of rum after Singh left, smiling wryly when I realized that it had not crossed my mind to ask him to stay for a drink. Was it really him or was it I who needed a lesson in acceptance?

The Sermon on Mountain Road

I pieced together this particular narrative from various sources, including a letter from a colleague, a colourful account in a local daily by a journalist with an active imagination, and a rambling, mirthful, but self-deprecatory question-answer session with JJ, the chief protagonist. While the comic aspects come out clearly in the account that follows, the deadly undercurrents are not that obvious. That the incident did not have a tragic ending can be put down not only to the extraordinary presence of mind displayed by JJ, but also to a large slice of luck.

The road from Kohima to Imphal is busy throughout the year as it carries almost the entire freight traffic needed to feed and provision the population of Manipur. Trucks groan along the winding mountain road, hauling their heavy load picked up at Dimapur or stations like Guwahati further beyond through the year. During the bitterly cold winter months the truck drivers looked like bandits of old, with great bandanas and woollen scarves covering their faces, leaving only a narrow slit for the eyes.

The day started innocuously enough with the group of high school boys and girls laughing as they hopped on to their bicycles and raced down the highway, some with guitars strapped on their backs, others with harmonicas in their pockets. One had even brought along a set of bongos and his T-shirt proclaimed that Elvis was the king. They all wore the uniform of the youth of the age, that is blue jeans and white T-shirts, with the only variation being in the messages emblazoned on the shirts. Soon, the laughter disappeared down the road as the last of the bicycles vanished round a curve.

Further up the road, at the CRPF picket near the Nagaland border, a small convoy got ready to leave for Imphal. A platoon under the command of an inspector was to return to the battalion headquarters after the men were replaced by a relief platoon. They had been on duty for the past two months and looked forward to two weeks of rest in Imphal before returning to duty. The convoy consisted of three one-tonners and two jeeps. The inspector and his deputy were in the lead jeep, accompanied by a driver, while the rest of the men were in the one-tonners, with the other jeep bringing up the rear. After a final check and counting of heads, the convoy moved off in a grinding of gears and roar of engines. A few seconds later, the valleys and slopes with their dense forest cover had absorbed the last of the sounds, and it was as if there had never been any vehicles there.

Sounds of laughter and singing rose from the narrow valley along with the gurgling of a stream gambolling its way between rocks and boulders. The youngsters could be seen sitting on tree trunks or rocks, strumming guitars and singing popular songs that spoke of unrequited love and heartbreak. A few hardy boys had thrown off their T-shirts and were frolicking in the shallow pools, trying to impress the girls. The girls rolled up their trouser legs and waded out into the pools looking for fish and tadpoles, and to impress the watching boys with their charms. The more serious-minded ones sat primly apart, keeping an eye on the packed picnic lunch which lay wrapped in baskets.

Getting more adventurous, the boys explored upstream and were soon lost to sight as well as hearing. The girls went about whatever they were doing. It was then that two CRPF soldiers

A cattlehand at work early morning in a local dairy in Imphal; mini cow sheds like this supply milk to most households, 2008

Girl returning home from school on the outskirts of Imphal, 2005

Festive chhatris (ornamental umbrellas) festoon the front of many Meitei temples, 2009

Above: Local produce at Ima Kaithel/Sana Kaithel, popularly known as Ima Bazaar, a market primarily run by women, 2009; *Below*: Local fish at Ima Bazaar, 2005

During wedding preparations, varieties of leefans (baskets made of cane and bamboo) are used as trays, 2005

Traditional invites are created elaborately from small pieces of coconut on betel leaves placed on many layers of banana leaves cut round, 2005

chanced upon them at the stream. It appears that their jeep had stalled due to an overheated engine and, as it was bringing up the rear, this went unnoticed by the rest of the convoy which soon vanished down the road to Imphal. Upon discovering the cause of the problem, the soldiers pulled up to the side of the road, hefted jerry cans and started down to the stream which they could hear flowing noisily below. They did not see the bicycles hidden among the trees, and so were taken by surprise when they ran into the group of girls. Broad smiles grew on their faces as they saw the pretty girls in their fitting outfits, and they called out greetings in Hindi. The girls however panicked on seeing the soldiers and, running to the other side of the stream, huddled together in fear. The soldiers advanced towards the stream. The girls sensed this to be a threatening gesture and screamed. Soon, the entire bunch was screaming, while the soldiers continued to fill their jerry cans, laughing and at the same time trying to reassure them. There was little sign even then that events were about to take a deadly turn.

The four boys, upon hearing the screams, rushed back and saw the soldiers at the stream, with the girls huddled on the other side. Two of them rushed forward to confront the soldiers while the other two took off in the direction of the road. The two who had hurled themselves at the soldiers, fists flailing, were easily pinned down by the latter, who tried to explain that they had merely come down to the river for some water. The boys continued to protest and thrash about and it was all that the soldiers could do to restrain and prevent them from throwing stones and other missiles.

The other boys had meanwhile managed to make it to the road and, retrieving their bicycles, pedalled furiously to the village. Their breathless arrival and incoherent message resulted in a mob gathering in a trice, mounting bicycles and motorbikes, and rushing to the spot. When they arrived at the place where the jeep was parked, they deflated the tires and rushed to the stream. To the enraged mob, the scene down by the stream was sufficient to incite them to deadly fury, and they began to mercilessly thrash the soldiers who were quickly overwhelmed by the vastly superior numbers. After beating the soldiers till they were bloodied and unconscious, the mob dragged them to the road. The hotheads among the mob began speaking of a lynching and a tragic ending to the incident appeared to be imminent. One of them had grabbed an automatic weapon he found on one of the soldiers and loosed off a burst that harmlessly shredded branches and leaves high up in the nearby trees. Others quickly searched the vehicle and found the other soldier's weapon, and the situation started to take on a menacing aspect as the adrenalin began to flow through youthful veins with the discovery of the weapons.

A few miles up the road, JJ sat back in the jeep and once again marvelled at the scenic beauty on either side. Despite the clear felling of trees in evidence in several spots as locals sought to create space to plant their crops, the climate was so generous and the soil so rich that the forest soon reclaimed its own. He enjoyed this trip every time he motored to Imphal, and looked forward each time the prospect came up. JJ was definitely not your avid naturalist or birdwatcher always up at the crack of dawn in his walking shoes and field glasses to catch the early bird after the early worm. He valued his sleep and tried to get as much of it as possible, especially in the morning hours. When the four of us shared an E-type residential house in Imphal as probationers, the difficulty in assigning times for using the toilet and bathroom was considerably lessened by JJ snoring stertorously while we completed our morning ablutions. However, even JJ, as I mentioned earlier, could be stirred by the morning view of the colourful vistas passing by on either side of the road.

His dark face with curly hair, well-proportioned features and ever-smiling lips was a magnet for the girls, and, as pretty girls at Tadubi found one excuse or the other to land up at his room at the inspection bungalow where he was billeted during training, he must have been hard put to remember and obey his mother's injunctions against consorting with the opposite sex. We of course did not believe a word of his solemn assurances that he just accepted the gifts of fruit and vegetables they brought, offered them a cup of tea and sent them on their way with well-meant advice as from an elder brother. Elder brother forsooth!

JJ smiled as he remembered these and other pleasant things, and his attention had just been caught by a flash of colour high in the trees when he heard the burst of gunfire near at hand. Even to his inexpert ears, the sound was definitely not that of a poacher loosing off a round at some hapless animal or bird. As his driver turned the next corner, he had to apply the brakes hard to avoid the bicycles parked or fallen on the road around the grey-blue jeep. As JJ jumped out of the vehicle and moved towards the clump of people gathered around the jeep, he first thought there had been a mishap involving the military vehicle and a cyclist. However, it was only when he came nearer that he saw the bloodied figures of the unconscious soldiers.

Seeing him approach, and noting that he was not a local, some of the mob began to move menacingly towards him. One of them brandished the weapon he had seized from the soldier; JJ's blood ran cold when he realized that the fellow had little idea of the weapon, as the barrel swung past JJ to describe a dangerous arc around him. Trying to think of what to do, JJ ended up asking lamely what was going on. He got a brusque reply that the soldiers were caught molesting the girls and would now be punished for their crime. JJ tried again to elicit information about the incident, but to no avail. It was then that he realized what it was to deal with an enraged mob with blood lust in its collective head.

JJ's mind flashed to his days at Fatima Mata College in his home town, Quilon, in far-off Kerala, which suddenly seemed further away than ever. There had been an altercation between two groups of students about the students' union election that was round the corner. Hot words had been exchanged and tempers ran high. Someone grabbed another's shirt front, and the other,

an outsider apparently called in to bolster forces, whipped out
a wicked-looking knife. At this, the other side too magically
produced assorted weapons and it looked like there was going to
be a bloodbath. At this time, Father Motha, the elderly warden of
the hostel, appeared and, towering over the students in his spotless
white cassock, thundered about the evil that was abroad, about
the un-Christian behaviour he saw, and that the way of all evil
was open before them. However, he said, they could choose to be
civilized and throw away their weapons and talk. Father Motha's
sermon not only got the attention of the ringleaders, but gradually
drew them away from the violence that was about to be unleashed
as they responded – at first reluctantly but later with animation –
and put forward their respective cases to him.

JJ realized that he would have to do something on the lines
of what Father Motha had done in that episode. Almost without
thinking, he whipped out a little red book that he always carried
in his pocket and, brandishing it over his head, cried, 'My young
friends, what have you done? Who among you is responsible for
the terrible sin of injuring your fellow men? Does not the Bible
forbid you from raising your hand against fellow man?' While he
spoke, he held the small book aloft, and the combination of his
raised, high-pitched voice, his fruity Malayalam accent and the
shiny little red book held high got him the attention he wanted. By
focusing on the perpetrators of the violence, he managed to drive
a wedge between them and the rest of the crowd that had gone
along. The crowd fell back in the face of his righteous Christian
anger; the killing light in the people's eyes seemed to wane and
fizzle out even as some among them recognized JJ, having seen
him about the little town of Tadubi, or at church singing loudly in
his enthusiastic and not entirely tuneful Malayali style. Those with
weapons of assorted descriptions tried to put them furtively out
of sight, and others tried to wipe bloodied hands clean on leaves
and grass.

Realizing that he had seized the advantage, JJ began firing on all cylinders, desperately seeking to keep the words coming in a torrent, and to lace his speech with authentic-sounding quotes and biblical metaphors. The crowd had fallen back to give him room, and the people now listened with downcast faces and abashed expressions as he ranted and raved about the evil acts they had committed and the awful punishment that awaited them in hell for what they had done. The girls had by now climbed up from the stream, and began to explain to the assembled crowd what had actually happened, that the soldiers had not done anything to harm them. Soon recriminations were flying fast and furious as each of the ringleaders tried to evade responsibility for what happened. JJ decided to let them stew in their own discomfiture for a while, and stood watching with a sardonic expression. As he expected, the ringleaders soon ran out of explanations and ideas, and turned to him for guidance as the enormity of their actions and the terrible retribution they were in for sank in. JJ now took charge of the situation, with erstwhile mob being reduced to just a crowd of confused and frightened youngsters.

The crisis having apparently passed, JJ realized he had to get the injured men urgent medical attention, because one of them appeared to be in bad shape. He also knew that he would have to try to manage the situation carefully to avoid bloody reprisals that would inevitably follow once the colleagues of the injured soldiers at the CRPF base heard about what happened. It was always the aftermath of such incidents that was the most difficult to manage, once the hot blood had cooled down and cold reality began to set in.

He organized the young people into groups and assigned them tasks, some to go to the stream and fetch water to give the injured, some to tend to them, and some to get cloth to dress their wounds. A young man was found who could drive the jeep, and laying the injured in it, the vehicle was instructed to be taken to the district hospital at Tadubi so that the men could get medical attention fast. The rest of the youngsters were told to go home, but not to forget about the incident. They were warned that the security forces would be back, looking for the leaders, at which information whatever bravado remained in the boys swiftly vanished into the air. The worried expressions on several faces and the hasty consultations indicated that the chief emotion shared by most in the crowd was one of shame and fury at having allowed themselves to be taken over by unthinking anger. JJ decided that such feelings would have their uses in the work he would have in future for some of these young men, and decided to make a note of the names of the leaders.

After the vehicle roared away, the rest of the crowd dispersed, and JJ found himself and his driver alone again in the silent forest. He started to tremble violently as the realization of the terrible tragedy that had been narrowly prevented came upon him with redoubled force. He hugged himself to stop his shaking, and tears rolled down his cheeks as he understood that divine providence had acted to prevent a lynching and its terrible consequences. He thanked God for giving him the opportunity to put his faith to the test for a good cause, and now set his imaginative mind to finding a way of ensuring the CRPF did not embark on a course of vengeance, that inevitably included requests for curfew in the affected village, house-to-house searches, detentions, beatings, disappearances or deaths in 'encounters'.

It was not going to be easy. Even in cases where there was good cause for trouble between the locals and soldiers, the CRPF would extract its pound of flesh. In this incident, soldiers had been brutally beaten while they were engaged in a harmless activity. More than a matter of wrongful beating, this about the 'locals' beating up soldiers who had been sent to keep the peace. Passions ran high even among senior officers when this aspect came up during discussions of military–civilian clashes.

As his vehicle sped through the forest, he sat back comfortably, catching glimpses of the blue sky when the tree canopy overhead parted. It was then that he realized that he was still clutching the red 'Bible' that had been used to such effect – his pocket diary that he always carried with him to note down things, lest he forget!

And thus was born the legend of JJ's 'Sermon on the Mountain'.

My First Transfer

I sat back in my chair and stretched. It had been a long day in the office. Since I took over as SDO of Ukhrul barely three weeks ago, this was the first day that I was spending almost wholly in office without stepping out for meetings or on an inspection or tour. It is not for nothing that what is called elsewhere as a work plan is referred to as the 'tour programme' in the civil services. The day spent working exclusively in the office allowed me the opportunity to witness the quotidian happenings of a minor government office. I regret not being able to report any sensational developments, stirring stuff that would keep the reader riveted.

That day, I got a taste of the fact that most of the busy but brief office work of a field officer in the revenue department (who spends most of his time rushing about on mostly useless inspections that generally end up interfering with what little work is done by lower functionaries) is spent asking those lower down in the hierarchy to furnish reports on every subject imaginable. This may look like productive work, but actually ends up creating work for others, which in turn interferes with their original assigned work. At the time, however, I don't think the real import of my discovery dawned on my then still-slowly-awakening awareness of my work and role as a junior officer of the government.

My presence in the office the whole day obviously meant that the others too had a day that was quite unlike the usual. Judging by their drawn faces, it had been an exhausting day, with unaccustomed effort having to be put in by all. The normally cheerful and relaxed air had become strained, and there was a palpable tension in the air. The usually cheerful and urbane superintendent felt the burden of the day most keenly, because he was the one who had the least to do when the SDO was away 'on tour'.

Once the news that I planned to be in the office all day to attend to office work permeated all parts of a shocked office, anxious enquiries were made to various quarters to fathom the reason for this change from a time-honoured practice of SDOs thoughtfully spending most of their time attending meetings at the DC's office or touring and inspecting far-flung villages and development projects. No one appeared to have an explanation for this extraordinary departure from tradition, and a sense of despondence descended on the staff. The skies also seemed to reflect this change of mood, and the day took on a brooding aspect, with the tension, like the humidity, rising steadily through the day, growing more oppressive by the hour, as the minutes ground heavily by. Everyone was certain that something bad was going to happen.

I started with the 'dak' or the correspondence file. This turned out to be a voluminous file folder with its contents not 'filed' but merely placed in the folder. A brief look revealed what I should have known all along: many letters were still to be replied to, reports remained to be completed and sent, and progress on matters to be done at subordinate offices awaited follow-up. In short, the work was very much in arrears. This appeared not to have happened all of a sudden or even recently, but looked to be the accretion of weeks and months of neglect.

The practice followed in that office for dealing with such matters appeared to have been born out of a combination of expediency and cunning forethought. If several reminders came on a particular matter, and if they appeared to grow in shrillness and urgency, an interim reply – usually couched in such soothing but bland

(and meaningless) terms that the reply was meant to accomplish little more than reassure the addressee that his concern was fully understood and that the matter was receiving the highest priority at the SDO's office – was drafted for the SDO to sign. If the matter concerned something that was referred by the local Member of Legislative Assembly (MLA), who happened in this case to also be the CM, then it would be red-flagged to ensure that it was acted on immediately. If it concerned any pecuniary benefit accruing to the petitioner, it was assigned high priority since this meant the prospect of additional income for the officials involved. All other matters had very little chance of getting done, and were thrown into a pile without even a mention in the ever-important 'inward' register. If anything is not listed in the 'inward', it does not exist.

A quick review of the situation convinced me that I had to start at the very beginning, and this meant that I had to start with the mail-handling process. In order to understand the significance of this seemingly innocuous and routine activity a word of explanation may be needed for the uninitiated. As the reader is no doubt aware, every matter that involves the government requires a 'file' to be in existence, testifying to the fact that the matter indeed exists. The file itself, that most sacrosanct of government documents, comes into existence once any matter is consigned to paper in the form of a petition, or complaint, or application. Upon it being received at the office to which it was addressed, it will be entered in the 'inward' register. Once it has been entered, it is doubtful whether there is any authority in the land that has the wherewithal to remove it from the register. That dastardly act is tantamount to striking a citizen's name off the Register of Births, thereby effectively extinguishing his corporeal presence on earth. After it has been entered in the inward register, the office superintendent decides whether it is a matter that is part of a file already in existence. This is usually decided by the simple artifice of looking for any reference in the letter to a prior file number. If such a reference is absent, it will be concluded that this is a fresh matter, and a new file will be opened. The latter may in all probability refer to a prior file, but considering the casual scrutiny to which the letters are subjected, one should not be surprised at the rapidity with which files appear to multiply like rabbits. This helps to support the argument for creating more posts in government offices, to deal with this deluge of work!

When I asked for the office manual in order to see for myself the procedure to be followed in dealing with incoming mail, I was greeted with a strained silence. As the silence deepened, and I felt I detected something like total incomprehension, I realized that I had asked for something that could not be provided. A couple of telephone calls soon procured a copy of the district manual from the DC's office and, before long, the superintendent and I had drawn up a rudimentary procedure to handle the recording and registering of all letters that arrived at the office. After impressing upon the superintendent that this should be done strictly every day, I also informed him that I would personally like to check the register every day. The superintendent took this announcement without flinching, although it was clearly a vote of 'low confidence' on his capacity to carry out instructions.

That matter having been dealt with, I reviewed the work allocation process in the office, and discovered that I had turned over a boulder under which had sheltered various kinds of strange and wonderful creatures that came crawling out, blinking at the unaccustomed light and disturbance. There were many in the office, with impressive-sounding designations, who appeared to have very little or no work of any kind. What the many files on their desks were seemed to be one of those things that had no reasonable explanation, since those worthies did not appear to know what was in the files, or how they got there, or what to do with them. It appeared to be more a case of having files on one's table as a symbol of the fact that the person behind the desk was important, the importance being directly proportional to the number of heaps of files that reposed on a person's desk.

Since most of the work related to programmes involving distribution of benefits of different kinds to various categories of eligible people, it was clear that tracking these matters was an important work in the hill areas. I decided to assign that work to a person identified by the superintendent as the most hardworking and honest fellow in the office. This man was given an assistant, selected again on the basis of capacity for hard work and reasonable honesty. In the same way, other work pertaining to magisterial matters, revenue appeals and related subjects was assigned to persons identified for their ability to write legibly and understand somewhat the subject at hand. All other subjects were to be directly handled by the superintendent, assisted by an LDC. The superintendent, although he tried valiantly not to show it, was dismayed at having to actually work after all those years of striding purposefully at a measured pace about the place like a colossus with enormous responsibilities but with very little to do. I also resolved to look into the filing system (that could charitably be described as whimsical, and less charitably, as without any logic) personally till some semblance of order had been imposed on it.

During the course of the day, while the work was being understood and allocated, I came across a file which the superintendent indicated was tagged 'most urgent' according to the system then prevalent for determining priorities at the time. An examination of the file revealed that it concerned the selection of beneficiaries for the local variant of the Antyodaya Programme, a well-meaning poverty alleviation scheme aimed at targeted intervention. It was based on identifying the poorest of the population of the district and ensuring that various benefits forming part of the programme actually reached them. On paper at least, this was one way to prevent or at least minimize the leakage of resources from poverty alleviation programmes. But, like many other such well-intentioned programmes, this too was subverted by the simple expedient of the politician-bureaucrat coalition drawing up the list of beneficiaries on the basis of their own criteria, which usually were simple and easily understood. Belonging to one's own village and tribe topped the list, followed by other less important factors. Of course, the fact that one was from the same village as the politician or bureaucrat did not exempt one from the time-honoured obligation to pay a tithe to the officials as a quid pro quo for getting one's name on the list.

The benefits that flowed to those fortunate to get their names on the final list ranged from cash amounts to items like sewing and knitting machines, household utensils, goats and cattle.

There is an anecdote about one such scheme, involving the distribution of a high-yielding variety of cow to the beneficiaries. The lucky ones attended the grand function arranged to distribute the largesse, received their mooing, plump cows and walked off, happily leading their cud-chewing gifts. The BDO and his staff fondly pictured each such family starting to earn money from the milk it sold each day, this money accumulating steadily in the bank, till one day, the family would build a small house from its earnings and invite the BDO and his staff over for a sumptuous meal of pork and sticky rice. On an inspection of that particular village several weeks later, the BDO came across one of the beneficiaries and enquired about the cow. The man was full of praise for the beast. This increased the BDO's sense of gratification. He then thought that it would be a good idea to see how the cow was faring, and looked forward to seeing a fat heifer with heavy udders so that he could suggest ways of further improving its yield. So he asked the villager to take him to the cow. The other worthy, on hearing the request, looked puzzled at first, and then burst into a peal of laughter and said, 'We ate it, my friend. The meat was excellent. The village talks of that feast even now!'

In another case, a young BDO set about identifying a list of people to be given a knitting machine. The selected persons were asked to come on a particular day and collect their machines, and a small ceremony was drawn up with the SDO present to give away

the machines. The photographer was in attendance, as were the
village headman and other 'red blankets'. The appointed hour came
and went, but there was no sign of the lucky villagers selected for the
government's munificence. Finally, the function was cancelled, and
an angry BDO demanded an explanation from his staff.

He was then informed that he had omitted to take the blessings
of the local parish priest before announcing the event, and should
have invited the man of God to bless the function. Without this,
the villagers would simply not come, for fear of offending the
priest, and through him, the church. The BDO had to swallow his
pride and his religious views and request the parish priest to bless
the programme. Once this was done, the programme proceeded
without a hitch!

It did not take me long to figure out that the file in front of
me represented another such government programme ripe for the
plucking. The fact that the system was being abused was evident to
the meanest intelligence, and I resolved to do something about it.
There was little ambiguity about the target group the programme
intended to help. But in the absence of a clear process to identify
beneficiaries, circumventing the good intentions of the initiators
of the programmes seemed quite easy. This shortcoming could be
corrected. I drew up a set of simple, easy to understand criteria
to be employed for selecting beneficiaries, and after running
through it a few times, and being rather pleased about it, I called
the superintendent in and explained it to him. His face lit up in
admiration at my initiative, and he shook my hand warmly to
show his appreciation. He nodded enthusiastically when I asked
him whether the system I had devised would be reasonably useful
in identifying the worthy beneficiaries without making the process
too bureaucratic or complicated. I then asked him to draw up a list
of people to recommend for the scheme based on the criteria I had
just drawn up.

With a helpful smile, he reached over for a slender file and
handing it to me, said that there was no need to take the trouble

since the list had already been prepared. I was surprised to learn this and enquired about the procedure followed. He explained that it had been drawn up by the minister's half-brother who was the vice chairman of the hill development council of the district, and that this was the time-honoured practice. I was not too pleased at the explanation and instructed him sharply to select the beneficiaries based on my system, and to bring it for my signature within an hour. I wanted the list to catch the last bus that left for Imphal in the evening, which took the last postal clearance in the mail bag too.

The superintendent protested that my proposition was not wise, and I believe he had my best interests at heart. This, however, did not improve my temper, and I raised my voice and ordered him to complete the task in the manner instructed by me. With a reproachful look, and seemingly hurt, he took the rejected list and retreated to his office to reappear within the hour with a fresh one. I quickly scanned the new list and was satisfied that it was done in accordance with the procedure laid down. It was typed once the spellings were checked, and after affixing my signature, it was sealed into an official-looking khaki cover and sent to the post office, where it caught that evening's post bag to Imphal.

I looked back on the day with a sense of satisfaction at having addressed important matters concerning the functioning of the office, and not a little because I had done my bit to ensure that a government programme was given the chance of succeeding. I congratulated the superintendent and others who were still in the office at that late hour for having done a fine job, and after going though the careful process of locking up for the night, returned to my quarters for what I felt was a well-earned rest after a day of constructive work.

The next day dawned bright and clear, and I arrived early at the office, looking forward to another day's work. The previous day's experience had convinced me that the next few days would be better spent in getting to grips with basic office processes that appeared to have been neglected for a long time. I figured that if I got these processes on a sound footing, the work of the SDO would be considerably simplified and improved. I had planned out what I would tackle on that day, having decided to cancel or postpone my various engagements. After attending to some spillover work from the previous day, I got fully involved with the task I had set myself, and did not realize that the day had passed and it was evening once again. The superintendent had by now resigned himself to my missionary zeal, and had even begun to find his work interesting. The younger members of the staff had begun to come up with suggestions, some of which were quite interesting, and I made a note to look into them the next day.

In the late afternoon, the superintendent came in bearing the 'dak' file that contained the fresh mail that had arrived by the afternoon bus from Imphal. I leafed through the mostly khaki envelopes and saw one addressed to me by name, and bearing the seal of the CS, Government of Manipur. Opening it, I scanned the contents. They were brief and to the point, informing me that I had been transferred as SDO, Imphal West, with immediate effect, and that I was to hand over charge that very day and report to the deputy commissioner of Central District the next morning. It took some time for the import of the letter to sink in, and when it did, I realized that I had been transferred after spending just twenty-nine days in my first field posting as an IAS officer.

My mind slowly adjusted to this new reality, and to the change in my circumstances. Thoughts about having to pack my few belongings that evening, finding the packing cases in which to put them, disposing off the food articles purchased for the house and other mundane things connected with being transferred mingled with the images of the past few weeks: the booming voice of Father Mathew attired in his customary colourful outfits; the polite and polished DC; the lovely Tangkhul women dressed in the current

Western fashion that put even the women in the metro cities to shame; elderly 'red blankets' walking solemnly into my quarters bearing vegetables and the odd squawking chicken that they first deposited in the kitchen before returning to sip hot tea in the little living room; Apang and Nelson, the lambus who looked after the house and me.

It was difficult to believe that I had arrived in the town just twenty-nine days ago. It was my first posting, but I was already going through what many young IAS officers before me must have learnt to expect with every transfer – that queer tug at the heart exerted by a place that till a few months earlier was totally unknown, just another name on the map. This quick dropping of roots in strange places is something the British officers of the East India Company experienced.

I was secretly relieved at the short notice because that meant I did not have to go through the ordeal of send-offs and speeches. I would miss some of the people, including the stately superintendent; the eager-to-please clerks; the willowy Tamsingphui with her striking sarongs; the loyal lambu who sat at my door, readily admitting every passer-by with a smile and a greeting, without finding out what they wanted, which was why he was placed there; and many others. I would of course inform the two priests and, knowing them, would probably end up finishing a bottle of Old Monk that evening with them. The convent's chubby Mother Superior – with her Malayalam-accented maternal clucking that made me feel homesick – would probably arrive with her brood of young nuns, with offers of help to pack.

These and other thoughts went through my mind as I filled out the TR-2 form that would be countersigned by the ADM, so that I could present it at the district treasury at Imphal and draw a fresh pay slip there to collect my monthly cheque. That chore done, I looked around a last time, checked the desk drawers once again for any personal effects, shook hands with the staff members who still remained at that hour, and stepped out into the street.

I walked down the few steps to the waiting jeep and, without a backward look, was driven off into the darkness.

Was I transferred because I chose to ignore the list prepared by the minister's brother? That appeared to be the most obvious explanation, although the speed of the reaction was unexpected and indeed shocking. Or was it part of the imminent (but still under wraps) shake-up in the administration of the valley where the government had apparently decided to crack down on the growing insurgency? When I asked him, the home secretary (HS) gave the latter explanation for the events. He explained that with the impending dismissal of the government on the grounds of breakdown of law and order in the valley, new people had to be inducted into key posts such as SDM, Imphal West, and SDM, Imphal East. As I came to understand the ways of government and governance in Manipur better, I believe it was probably a case of killing two birds with one stone! I don't believe I had managed to demonstrate my administrative capabilities in twenty-nine days at Ukhrul so as to convince the higher-ups that I was the right man for the job. Since tough decisions were to be taken in the valley, the simple expedient was to remove Meitei incumbents (whose loyalties were suspect) from these sensitive posts and replace them with mayangs like me who could be 'trusted'!

But in Ukhrul, my sudden transfer would surely come to be held up as an example of the swift retribution that followed an officer's ill-advised decision to ignore the wishes of powerful people and to follow his own ideas.

Tea with the Governor

$\mathcal{A}$

The courtroom buzzed with the sounds of many conversations taking place in low voices, traffic moving about on the road outside the DC's office compound, typewriters clacking away in unseen office rooms, crows cawing noisily, children laughing on their way back from school, bystanders lounging about in the veranda or in the corridors of the court, waiting for their cases to be called – in short, another typical day in the court of the SDM, Imphal West.

I turned to the bench clerk, Manikanta Singh, and asked him to call the next case. He peered at the case diary in front of him and intoned the number of the next case, hearing which, two lawyers seated among others of their profession in the long benches provided to them started to rouse themselves from the torpor into which they had fallen, gather their papers, clear their throats, and go through all the motions prior to doing the work for which they had been hired by the anxious-looking petitioners hovering around. The bench clerk rose to inform me of the status of the case when the orderly who sat outside the room in which I sat on a raised platform, entered and said in an urgent undertone that the DC wanted to see me immediately. Deciding that it must be something important, I adjourned the court for the day, requested the bench clerk to fix fresh posting dates and hurried out.

It took me some time to cover the distance to the DC's office, which was located to the far side of the sprawling single-storeyed structure that was the DC's office complex.

The orderly hurrying ahead cleared the way through the throng that usually gathered during a working day at this building, and soon I was ushered into the quiet but spacious office of my boss, the urbane deputy commissioner of Central District. A burly handsome man in his mid-fifties, the DC radiated power and strength from his strong square face, broad shoulders, and barrel-chested form. He was well dressed as usual, with grey flannels and full-sleeved shirt with tie and a sleeveless sweater; a coat lay over the arm rest of the chair in front of the desk. There were three rows of chairs in front of the desk. Usually they were full, as delegations of various kinds poured out their problems to him. He always listened to these patiently, chewing slowly on the paan that was ever present in his mouth, but with no trace of red on his lips. The beautiful silver paan box stood open on his desk, and I could see fresh betel leaves neatly stacked in one compartment, a wad of tobacco in another, a little round container with a lid for the lime paste, and other ingredients that went into making of the fastidious man's paan. That day, however, the room was empty, and he appeared to be waiting for me. Gesturing to me to sit down, he continued to chew methodically for some time, till I realized that he was waiting for someone else to arrive. The curtains parted and my colleague, NM, who was the SDO, Imphal East, briskly marched in and greeted the DC.

Without much ado, the DC said, 'You are both wanted at the Raj Bhavan. His Excellency the governor wishes to meet both of you. Your appointment is at 1215 hours. This means that you have just enough time to go home, change into your band galas and be there at least ten minutes before the appointed time. The CS, HS and I will be there as well, but apparently the old man wants to talk to the two of you separately. Naturally, we are all curious about this, and I am sure you will give us a good account of the meeting after it is over.' Smiling his usual half smile, he rose, and with a gesture of dismissal, sent us on our way.

We rushed to our respective quarters and, pulling on the black band galas that had lain neglected since the Mussoorie days, managed to reach the Raj Bhavan almost at the same time. As we alighted near the gate, still wiping traces of dust from our clothes, and reported to the aide-de-camp (ADC) there, we could see several cars and police jeeps, all bearing stars and flags indicating that most senior officials in Imphal were already there. We were followed by curious stares as we self-consciously walked in our formal attire through the throng of distinguished officials. As we entered, we could see the CS and the HS in conversation to one side of the large hall. Seeing us, the CS called us over to where he stood and said, 'Glad you chaps could make it in time. The old man hates it when people are late. Let me see your attire. What a terrible fit and cut! I'm sure it must be that blasted Hari's work. Anyway, too late to do anything about it. I should have checked you chaps out earlier. This will definitely not help the old man's mood. Anyway, there's nothing to be done but to face the music like men.' On that cheery note, he advised us to sit still, not fidget, and answer the questions to the point and in a clear voice. He said that the ADC would have briefed the governor about us, so we need not introduce ourselves.

The door to an adjacent room opened and the ADC stepped out. Seeing us with the CS, he walked over and addressed the CS: 'His Excellency will see them now, sir.' The CS sat back, looked us over again and shook his head, but managed a grim smile and said, 'Good luck, chaps.' The ADC went back into the room, and we followed. The door closed quietly, and we found ourselves standing in a room which looked like a small library or a large study. Across the thick carpet was a writing table, behind which sat the governor, reading something. He looked up briefly over the reading glasses at us, gestured to us to be seated, and continued with his reading, while the large grandfather clock counted the moments. After a couple of minutes, he was done and, closing the file, he looked at us seated opposite him, stiff in our black band galas. He muttered, 'These suits of yours must be the handiwork of … what's the fellow's name, the chap in Mussoorie? Ah, yes, Hari. They're badly tailored, and if I were you, I would get rid of these suits and get myself a better-tailored outfit.'

He enquired about where we were from, what our fathers did, how we found life and work in Manipur, about the training at the academy. All this was done in a dry, deep and soft voice, so that one had to strain one's ears not to miss out on what he was saying. Even seated, it was clear that he was a very tall man, reputedly standing over six feet four inches in his socks. With his great height, fair complexion, bald head and large beak-like nose, he bore a striking resemblance to Charles de Gaulle. If rumours were to be believed, his ways were no less imperious. In fact, it was famously said that when he was the Union home secretary and there was a disagreement between him and the home minister, it was the latter who had to resign! More recently, he was credited with the memorable epitaph on the bureaucracy during the Emergency: 'All that was asked of you was to bend; but you crawled!'

It was quite intimidating to be seated in a smallish room across such a powerful personality. To add to this, in Manipur, the governor was not just the titular head of government in the sense that governors of other states were, with largely of a ceremonial nature. He was the governor of all the north-eastern states and had establishments in each state, although he spent most of his time in Shillong where the North-Eastern Council (of which he was chairman) was located. What made his position even more important for us was that the Shaiza government had just been dismissed earlier that day, and president's rule promulgated in the state. There was an air of expectancy about the place as decisive action was expected to be initiated by the governor to reign in insurgency which had gotten out of hand under the previous government. The state administration was gearing up to take corrective steps to set right the mistakes made by the previous government. This meant that key posts would be reassigned, with favourites of the erstwhile dispensation being eased out to minor positions, and others being moved in. Two advisors had been named, men who would enjoy formidable powers as long as president's rule was in force. Their arrival was expected in a couple of days.

The governor looked at us keenly and asked us whether we were scared about the insurgent activity in our area. We had prepared for just such a question, and had decided to be honest in our answers. We admitted that we were not fully used to the idea that we would be targets of the underground, although we knew that the insurgent activity had been on the rise in the valley. He then bluntly asked, 'Do you need a gunman to accompany you in your work?' This was another query we knew would come from some high quarters at some stage, and we had spent time discussing this among ourselves. We answered that we did not feel it would be of much use. I recall imagining the efforts of the gunman trying to disentangle himself from his ancient Enfield rifle in the cramped rear seat of the jeep, while unseen insurgents took potshots at us! More importantly, we felt that the presence of a gunman would actually attract attention to us.

The governor digested what we had said. He appeared pleased, not so much in terms of his expression, but in view of what he said. 'It will be a sad day when even the district administration needs protection to go about its work. I'm pleased at your reply, which I think reflects the correct attitude. But, I want you young fellows to be careful and not take unnecessary risks. If the situation does deteriorate, I want you to ask for protection. Is that clearly understood?' We nodded and said, 'Yessir!' He stood up, unwinding his large frame slowly to its full height. He extended his hand and, shaking ours briefly, gestured in dismissal. As we left the room, we passed the CS, HS and DC going in, and the CS smiled at us, saying under his breath that we should meet him later at his office.

We stood in the sunlight, loosening the tight collar of the band gala, as well as a couple of the top buttons. I had clearly put on a little weight after leaving the academy. As we waited for our jeeps, I thought about the governor's parting words, and wondered how it would feel to have a gunman riding in the jeep with me as I went about my work. I decided that I would not be comfortable until I knew more about the person assigned the task of protecting me – how good he was with a gun, what kind of temperament he had, and related issues. I decided I would worry more about him than about getting shot by the insurgents. I felt we had done the right thing, and that we were better off without the gunman.

The silent corridors and high ceilings of the Raj Bhavan, together with the murmur of voices behind closed doors and the clacking of unseen typewriters and the clatter of a teleprinter, all gave off an aura of urgency and power. This was heady stuff, far removed from the dusty, crowded offices we had been hitherto exposed to, and we were quite excited. Suddenly, what we were doing seemed important, part of a grand purpose. We strode out with a spring in our steps.

The driver, Rajen Singh, jumped out of the jeep and looked around him, plainly impressed at being inside the Raj Bhavan for the first time. Seeing his reassuringly placid face, I decided I would be better off with Rajen around if confronted by insurgents. And with that thought, and the picture of Rajen's reaction in such an emergency bringing a smile to my lips, we drove off without the customary squeal of tyres, the surroundings having obviously made an impression on the man at the wheel, accelerating only when we were well clear of the imposing gates.

Curfew Supervision

❧

The news broke while I was in the courtroom, hearing a case. The assistant public prosecutor (APP) laboriously reviewed the flimsy evidence marshalled by him to establish the public nature of the pathway in dispute. His droning voice gave a queer feeling – as if the APP was a skilled ventriloquist whose voice alternately emanated from the fan overhead and from the sweaty, puffy face emerging from the starched lawyer's collar with its sweat stains. My attention began to wander to anything that could hold my attention long enough for my brain to focus on it – a stain on a shirt front, an unzipped trouser, or a lawyer vigorously scratching a very private part of his anatomy in full public view. The sleep centres would then settle down as my attention would home in on these edifying sights, while the counsel droned on. For me, this was the most difficult part of the courtroom procedure – staying awake while the lawyers did their interminable business.

I remembered reading somewhere that sleepiness in a crowded, poorly ventilated hall was less due to the soporific qualities of the speaker's content and delivery but had a lot to do with the concentration of positive ions in the room. As the positive ion concentration increased, so did the drowsiness. One way to counter this was to increase the negative ion count in the hall, and magically, the audience would find its drowsiness disappear! But such a device would be a mixed blessing in the courtroom as then we would be obliged to listen attentively to the uninspiring fare dished out by rival lawyers as they trawled at infuriatingly leisurely pace for inspiration or a fact that could turn the case.

The soothing voice that had merged into the background sounds like the drone of a tambura stopped all of a sudden. Like Justice Stareleigh in the immortal courtroom scene in *The Pickwick Papers*, I woke up, realizing that the APP had either paused, or concluded his arguments. I tried to look grave and judicial as I searched his perspiring face. He was gazing out of the window as if trying to locate the source of some distant sound that had impinged on his consciousness and transfixed him. I also looked at the defendant's lawyer for a clue about the next move. The latter appeared to have dozed off, with muted snores escaping his face that was sunk deep into his multiple chins. I then looked around at the bench clerk for assistance, and he pointed at the side door, where a messenger stood, eyes closed in apparent ecstasy, scratching his groin with an official-looking envelope in his hand, the reason for the APP's pause. I adjourned the case for five minutes and left the courtroom to read the message. It was a terse one from the DC, informing me that the governor had dismissed the Government of Manipur and that president's rule had been declared in the state. I was to report immediately to the DC's office where an urgent meeting would be held to discuss arrangements to be taken in the light of these developments.

Returning to the courtroom, I announced that the court would not sit for the rest of the day due to unforeseen developments, and that fresh posting dates would be announced by the bench clerk. As the lawyers and their clients collected their files and papers and gathered around the clerk's desk to negotiate suitable posting dates, the murmur of conversation grew till it was the unmistakable and distinctively Indian sound of dozens of people speaking at the same time. I recalled an account by Garfield Sobers of playing a Test match before a full house at the Eden Gardens and presuming that the constant roar in the background was that of the sea. He learnt later that the sea was more than 100 miles away to the south, and what he heard was 80,000 Indians speaking simultaneously! I left the babel behind and hurried across to my office through litter-ridden corridors. I decided to collect my files, diary, and attaché case, since it appeared highly probable that I would not return to the office that day.

I was among the earliest to arrive, and was soon joined by the ADM, the other SDOs, and some other officials who had converged from various corners of the sprawling collectorate building. Like most of the meetings convened by this DC, this one too was brief and to the point. A man of few words, he spoke deliberately, with well-chosen sentences. He never repeated himself, neither out of habit nor for rhetorical effect, and this little characteristic of his stayed with me for a long time. It was almost as though he was reading out from a prepared, edited text. In his usual telegraphic style, he informed the group that prohibitory orders were to be promulgated with immediate effect in Central District, and that the city would be placed under dusk-to-dawn curfew from 5 p.m. onwards. A thrill of excitement shot through me as I contemplated my first curfew, with images of deserted streets, police vehicles on patrol, and a taut sense of expectation.

After the meeting, we drove to the secretariat, where we were taken to another meeting convened by the CS, at which senior police officers were present in strength, all in uniform for a change – a clear sign that this was not business as usual and that something big was afoot. Using a large map of the city and a long pointer, the DIG, Operations (Ops), explained the arrangements for enforcing the curfew – the zones into which the city had been divided, and which police or paramilitary outfit would be responsible for each. After this briefing, the CS took over, and observed that curfew was being imposed in the valley after an interval of many years, and it was likely that people had forgotten what it meant. In order that it serve the purpose for which it had been imposed, it was necessary that curfew be implemented effectively. Therefore, he wanted teams comprising one officer from the DC's office and one from the police to monitor the enforcement of curfew; this would be reviewed daily at a meeting convened personally by the inspector general of police (IGP). Unusual arrangements indeed.

We left the meeting room and deciding that we did not have time to go home for a late lunch, opted to grab a bite at the Airlines Hotel in the bazaar. While we ate, we were joined by the owner, a thick-set Punjabi who never missed an opportunity to fraternize with government officials. After the customary exchange of greetings, I was appalled when a colleague continued the discussion of the security arrangements in the presence of the newcomer. On seeing my raised eyebrow and theatrical rolling of eyes, the officer gestured that it was all right, and calmly continued. Seizing the opportunity afforded by a pause, the restaurant owner exclaimed, 'I'm glad curfew is being imposed. That will teach these insurgents and their sympathizers a thing or two. The bastards have been getting too uppity of late, threatening us businessmen and extorting money from us. I'd like to see their faces now.' His glee was difficult to miss, and I suddenly felt a diminishing of the enthusiasm with which I had been looking forward to enforcing the curfew. Irritation flared as a thought struck me: *Does the chap think the curfew rules do not apply to him?* There was something about his ingratiating manner that repelled me, a vague feeling that he felt he was one among us – that 'we' were on the same side. I did not enjoy the lunch much after that.

It was nearing 4 p.m. when we returned to the secretariat, waiting for the police officers who were to form the other half of our respective observer teams. We were to travel in well-marked police vehicles, which was a big relief because I had visions of my dusty, faded jeep driven by the redoubtable Rajen Singh being slow to heed a warning at a police picket and the resulting hail of gunfire cutting us to ribbons. The affable assistant inspector general (AIG) at the police headquarters walked over, and the two of us climbed into the vehicle waiting for us. I was glad that I would be with this pleasant chap for this task. We were assigned a zone in a part of the city that comprised largely commercial areas. However, like all commercial areas in the north-east, the shops had their living quarters on the upper floor, with their owners staying upstairs. Commercial streets therefore filled up, after hours, with owners – mostly Marwaris – and their families and other mainlanders, with very few locals to be seen. After the business during the day being conducted mostly in Meitei, the evening would bring Hindi. It was nearing 5 p.m., which was when the curfew would take effect, but the people appeared unhurried as they went about their shopping and other chores, even as police vehicles with public address systems went around blaring stern warnings about the curfew rules, and advising the public to get back home before the curfew set in.

Our watches now showed that it was 5 p.m. In a few minutes, the town had fallen eerily silent, with no vehicles on the roads, which was an unusual sight because the streets were always filled with the omnipresent bicycles and rickshaws. It was already dark, and the street lights already lit. Our vehicle was soon the only one on the roads. The jeep moved slowly, the driver aware that sudden moves would lead to trouble. As we rounded a curve, a lone dark figure detached itself from the shadows of the shop awnings and moved to the middle of the street. It was a soldier in full gear, with an automatic weapon held loosely in one hand. With his other hand he gestured to us to stop, and continuing to use his hands in universal sign language, signalled us to dowse the headlamps, switch on the cabin lights, and to step out with our hands clearly visible.

The tension was palpable. While I had seen such scenes many times in the movies, the hollow feeling in the pit of the stomach that I had read about in books soon manifested itself. And although it was quite cold, I found myself breaking out into a sweat. It was amazing that I, an officer of the government, with powers to arrest people and throw them in prison, and very much part of the establishment, should feel so vulnerable despite travelling in a well-marked police jeep, accompanied by police officers! This is what happens when the familiar things we take for granted are removed, when one finds oneself in a street facing a soldier with a weapon. Suddenly, there are no rules or positions of authority – all the cards are held by the man with the gun.

Trying to move as slowly as I could, I followed the AIG out into the street, noting that the driver had complied with all instructions. When we were clear of the vehicle, the soldier came forward and asked us for our ID papers, which we produced, remembering to move slowly and keep our hands visible while they went to our pockets to retrieve the ID cards. These were examined using a flashlight the soldier had produced, and he returned them with a smart salute. With this came a vast feeling of relief, as if by magic, the suddenly unfamiliar landscape had vanished to be replaced by the familiar objects and relationships.

At this, more shadows detached themselves from the darkness on either side of the street, and I had my first experience of how soldiers manned a checkpoint. We had been covered by soldiers invisible to us from the moment we turned into that street, and were only a finger squeeze away from being riddled with bullets if we made a false move. The sweat congealed on my back, my shirt clinging damply to my skin, as we climbed back into the vehicle, the AIG not forgetting to utter a 'Shabaash!' that brought a smile to the section leader of the detachment we had just encountered.

We spent the next hour and a half slowly covering every street in the zone assigned to us, and our experience was the same at every checkpoint. The competence of the CRPF soldiers manning the checkpoints impressed me, and after the first couple of checkpoints, my nervousness started to wane as I felt reassured by their calm air of competent toughness. At one checkpoint, we saw three young men being frogmarched into a nearby building, one of them held brutally by his hair by a large soldier who admonished them as they were dragged away: 'You thought the warnings were for fun, did you? We'll teach you to know better in future.' Thudding sounds followed by cries and screams from inside the building indicated that the instruction was swift and harsh. Then there was silence, as the unfortunate curfew violators would be left for the night to ponder over their foolishness at ignoring the warnings.

These were usually young men having a good time, some probably with a couple of drinks sloshing around inside them. I tried to imagine their feelings as they sat in shocked silence, nursing bruises and aches, wondering about what had happened. Their fear would be mixed with anger and loathing for the soldiers responsible, for the hated mayangs who decided when they could walk the streets of their own towns and villages. A sure way to ensure a supply of willing recruits for the underground, I could not help thinking.

As we drove off, I was shaken by the suddenness and brutally effective nature of the punishment, and the absence of anger on the soldier's face as he beat the young violators. The soldiers were just doing their job, it appeared, and they were intent on doing it well. They were far from home, missed their families, and their customary food and sounds and smells, felt the cold and the alienness of their surroundings keenly, and took all this out on the hapless violators. The sickening sounds of knuckles meeting bone and flesh, of the sharp reports of slaps on faces and rifle butts thudding against ribs and jaws remained with me for a long time. I tried to tell myself that this was necessary for the curfew to be effective, but found it difficult to convince even myself. The AIG and I looked at each other, as though the same thought were going through our minds, and then we looked away hastily, as if ashamed of such thoughts.

I was beginning to get into the spirit of curfew enforcement when everything almost came undone at the next checkpoint.

As our vehicle approached another road junction, we saw an astonishing sight. Strung in an even line across the road, clearly visible in the brightly lit street under the sodium vapour lamp atop the high mast at the junction, stood what was obviously the entire cohort of ten men assigned to that checkpoint. We stared at this remarkable sight, my mind wildly thinking that this was what the poster of the film *The Magnificent Seven* looked like, when the driver stopped the jeep and waited for the usual instructions. Instead, what greeted our disbelieving ears and eyes was several hoarse voices emerging from wildly gesticulating figures bellowing different instructions all at the same time. The driver naturally panicked and forgot to switch off the headlamps, which appeared to enrage the men in the picket line across the road. The roared instructions and imprecations became even more blood-curdling as they climbed in pitch, indicating that some of them were getting nervous at our behaviour. I desperately looked out of the corner of my eye at the AIG, wondering what we should do, and I could see that he was trying hard to stay calm. One instinct was to burst out laughing at the theatrical scene in front of us, but that would surely have resulted in us being cut to pieces in a hail of bullets.

The men had their weapons at the ready, nervous fingers on triggers, the barrels vibrating like tuning forks in trembling hands, swinging them in a dangerous arc covering our vehicle and most of the portion of the street where we stood. The AIG and I moved away from the vehicle slowly, but even this did not appear to appease some of the men. As the seconds ticked menacingly by, we could finally discern – by his posture and swagger, as well as the fact that he wore a Stetson hat with one flap attached to the peak in the manner of Hindi film leading men – that the man in the middle of the line strung across the street was the ranking officer. He stood in the classic gunfighter pose made popular in film posters of the old Westerns: feet apart, hand hovering over the holster itching to draw his weapon, eyes narrowed as he sized up the target, a grim mirthless smile on his lips that were drawn back in a semi-snarl. He looked vaguely familiar, and finally it was the AIG who broke the silence saying in a low, curt voice: 'Mr Mukhopadhyay, please instruct your men to lower their weapons and to stop shouting so that one of them can approach and examine our ID papers.'

At these unexpected words spoken in a measured tone, the spell was broken, and the cold fear that had been crawling up my spine started to recede. The soldiers looked uncertain, shocked into silence by the AIG's quiet voice, and they looked to their superior for instructions. The latter slowly abandoned his gunfighter stance and asked in a loud voice: 'Who is that who spoke? Identify yourself at once!'

'AB, AIG (Ops) and CB, SDO, Imphal West. I suggest someone check our ID papers fast; otherwise I shall have to report a deviation from standard procedure at this checkpoint.' This last was said with some humour, which appeared to be totally lost on the officer, who now looked uncertain. He however came hesitantly forward and gestured to one of his men to check our papers. Having got close enough to recognize AB, the other said in a relieved tone: 'Hello, AB. Good to see you. How are things going this evening?'

'Quite well, so far,' the AIG replied shortly. 'Considering it is the first day, I must say the people have managed to get back to their homes without much problem. Luckily for you, we weren't terrorists. We could have picked off half your men before they could have fired a shot in return, standing as you were in the light and strung across the road.' The other laughed and tried to make light of the incident, but I wasn't laughing as I recalled the nervousness and fear in the voices of the soldiers as they bellowed instructions at us out of panic and uncertainty. I also learnt that even an ordinary weapon in the hands of an amateur and a scared person is the most dangerous thing you can be on the wrong side of!

We climbed back into the jeep, anxious to get as far away from that picket as soon as possible. We didn't speak as the driver manoeuvred the vehicle through a narrow stretch of road where some repair work was being done, and we were soon on our way back home after the checking was completed. We rode in silence, although we were out of the curfew-affected area and in the security zone where the officer quarters were located. We would be doing this again the next day, and parted at the gate of my quarters, AB driving off into the night.

The next day, I sat in my office, going through reports of the previous day's incidents. There had been many reports of curfew violation, as it had been many years since the people of the valley experienced curfew. The newspapers did not carry news of these as they were published not from Imphal but from Guwahati and Kolkata. What I was studying were the intelligence reports, and these showed that the first day's curfew had yielded a rich harvest of key figures of the underground taken unawares by the measure. I realized that this was probably done intentionally, with a view to getting key people separated from their teams, giving the security forces time to pick them up singly. Those who had been picked up were not yet formally arrested, and hence news of their disappearance would take a couple of days to filter back to their cadres. This would enable those caught to be interrogated, leading to more arrests. My friend Panditji and his crack commando team of 29 CRPF were at the forefront of this effort, while the smokescreen created by the curfew deflected attention from this objective.

The phone rang and it was a senior IAS officer with a wide circle of friends in Imphal. It turned out that he wanted me to issue curfew passes for his friends who had planned a big party and were taken unawares by the curfew order. I heard him out and said I would see what I could do. In less than an hour, a red-painted jeep sporting flashy accessories drew up outside my office with a screech of brakes and tyres, attracting the attention of the bystanders. The driver was soon announced. He was obviously the friend that the IAS officer had referred to earlier. He must have been in the room when the officer made the call. I looked up to see a fashionably dressed man in his forties, with the expression of one who knows his way about the place, and who can get things done in many ways. He sat down and, opening a pack of imported cigarettes, lit one and offered me the pack, which I ignored. He presently spoke: 'I have come about the curfew passes.'

'I'm sorry, you cannot get a pass because we are not issuing them except for security personnel and people having emergencies,' I answered quietly.

He smiled broadly and said, 'This *is* an emergency, my dear chap. The party has been planned for weeks in advance, and now I can't just cancel it. People are coming over from Kolkata and Guwahati. Everyone who is anybody will be there.'

'Then I'm afraid everyone will be disappointed.'

His tone changed, and he said that he came over because he thought I had agreed, and added that important people would not be happy at this development.

Something in me snapped at this, and images of the previous night rolled past my eyes – of young men being beaten for violating curfew, suspected insurgents and security forces locked in a deadly cat-and-mouse game, people on both sides of the law doing their chosen jobs with commitment and fear and heroism and desperation. And here was this smug fellow, grinning and worrying about his party.

'I suggest you leave, and make sure you are in your house or indoors somewhere by 5 p.m. I will be personally supervising curfew, and will be looking out for you. I know who you are, and I assure you that you will be picked up if you violate curfew. And, believe me, that will not be a very pleasant experience,' I said, standing up.

He got up and left without a word. This was definitely not the end of the matter, I realized. *But tomorrow is another day, and what the hell, maybe I'd get lucky and the bloke will get picked up tonight by a CRPF patrol!* I sat back in my chair, humming an old film tune, smiling as I imagined his red jeep with all the fancy fittings being stopped for curfew violation by a bunch of soldiers.

The Magisterial Enquiry

For the tenth time, I flipped through the pages of the voluminous file, trying in vain to find the references cited in the note file. Prominent flags decked the otherwise drab, dog-eared bunch of sheets, but other than slightly improving the appearance of the file, they did nothing by way of helping to navigate through the dense argument marshalled in favour of the proposal. With a sigh, I went back to the beginning, hoping to find some clues to the mystery there.

Bal Bahadur – the handsome young Nepali who had one day appeared at my door uninvited and unannounced, and who had developed into a manservant of exceptional quality – stuck his head between the curtains of the door leading to the veranda and announced that four people were waiting to see me. Puzzled because I was not expecting visitors, I put aside the file, secretly happy at any excuse to do so, and went out. I found four swarthy strapping young men standing in the kerchief-sized patch of grass, their close-cropped hair betraying their military connections. This was getting more curious, I thought as I went to the edge of the little veranda and stood looking at them. Despite the extra foot I gained by standing on the veranda, the men almost came up to my eye level as they straightened and smartly stood to attention, in the manner of soldiers out of uniform while acknowledging a senior.

'What can I do for you?' I enquired politely. They hesitated, looked at each other, and finally, with the urging of the others, one among them spoke.

'We are with the CRPF and are posted here at Imphal. We are from Kerala and wanted to meet you as we learnt you are from Kerala too.' This was said with a smile, which felt familiar, especially since it was accompanied by a particular Malayalam phrase. Not only was it the first time I had come across soldiers trying to fraternize on the basis of linguistic affinity, it was also unusual for them to visit an IAS officer's house to make their acquaintance. Although not suspicious by nature, I became alert and waited for them to speak, responding with just a half smile to the opening words of the one who had spoken. I tried to suppress what appeared to me to be a snobbish response to an apparently harmless attempt by some Malayali chaps very far from home to meet and chat up one of their own kind, but I was still somehow getting increasingly annoyed at their presumptuousness.

'We don't get to meet many Malayalis here, sir, and we thought it will be nice to meet you. We stay in this part of town, over there, past the DIG, Border Security Force (BSF) office,' one of them said. I did not respond to this and waited for them to go on, and realized that it was making them more nervous. My clean-shaven face, and absence of the usual pronounced Malayalam-accented English had already confused them, and they must have started to think there had been a mistake. The person who spoke first decided to find out.

'Sir, you are CB, the SDO, Imphal West, are you not?' I nodded. 'You are from Kerala, sir?' I nodded again. He volunteered the information that he was from Alleppey, and that the others were from other towns in Kerala. I smiled in acknowledgement of this information. Then, the conversation flagged and the silence grew again. I decided that I could not be more forbidding than I had already been, and spoke to them in Malayalam, upon which their mood improved and they smiled brightly, relieved that the awkward opening moments had been successfully negotiated. I asked Bal Bahadur to bring some chairs out to the veranda, and after we were seated and the tea poured, I decided to ask them whether they had any specific problem that brought them to my house. By now, thoroughly relaxed, and their guard down at my informal behaviour, they came straight to the point.

'You are conducting an enquiry into an alleged atrocity committed by the CRPF, sir. We are from the battalion involved. Many of the soldiers are Malayalis, and we are trying to do a tough job, far from home. The allegations are all fabricated and they will destroy the careers of good men. We came to request you to help these men.'

My smile vanished at these words and I stood up and requested them to leave the house. They got up confused, and stepped out into the patch of grass. I remained on the veranda.

'It would be best if you leave immediately. I don't know who put you chaps up to this little enterprise, but you should have known that it will only go against you. I don't remember your names, and it is a good thing, as I will forget that this ever happened. Otherwise, it might go badly against you, as well as the jawans involved. You may go now.' I waited while they shuffled out to the waiting jeep, which soon moved off in the direction of the CRPF encampment.

I went back inside after they left, but could not concentrate on the file that had previously engaged my attention. Abandoning my attempt to make sense of its convoluted reasoning, I shut it angrily and sat back, my mind going back to the curious meeting I had just had. I could see what must have happened to get them to pluck up the courage to come to my house. Their commanding officer, would have said, 'Arre, Nair, the SDO conducting the magisterial enquiry into the Singjamei incident is also from Kerala. Why don't you go meet him and get him to take a lenient view? And, while you are at it, take along a few other Mallus. Perhaps it will be a good idea to take along a couple of bottles of rum. I believe this young chap enjoys his drink.' I was already seething at this purely imaginary conversation when the telephone rang. I snatched the receiver off the rest with some irritation, and barked, 'Hello.'

A polite voice said, 'Am I speaking to Mister Balagopal, SDO, Imphal West?' I replied that he was indeed speaking to that person. The voice went on: 'I am Major Mishra. I would like to come over and apologize for the actions of a few of my men a short while ago. May I come and see you if it is convenient now?' My initial reaction was to refuse. However, swallowing my anger, I asked him to come over. A few minutes later, I heard the sound of a jeep drawing to a halt outside. Firm steps sounded on the hard ground before I heard a sharp knock on the door. I bade the officer enter, which he did briskly. I saw a stocky, powerfully built, square-jawed man dressed in what is called in the military 'PT' attire – white T-shirt, white shorts, white socks and white running shoes. Everything was sparkling white, and the crease on his shorts could have drawn blood: it was so sharp. He sat down on being invited to do so, sitting erect, and though he looked uncomfortable, I did not encourage him to relax.

I waited for him to speak, and he did, explaining that his men's action was unpardonable, that they were misguided by the advice of an officer, that the officer had been suitably reprimanded, and that he was personally requesting me to let the matter drop.

I reminded him that not only was an attempt made to influence a government official in the course of his duties, but this was even more serious since I was engaged in a magisterial enquiry, which amounted to an attempt to interfere with the workings of a court.

The visitor agreed with my assessment and remained silent, awaiting my decision. The silence grew till it was almost palpable. I finally said, 'Major Mishra, regarding this misguided attempt by your men, I will treat the matter as closed. Not because they are fellow Malayalis but because they are young men far from home trying to do a tough, thankless job. I think I know exactly how they feel. But I too have a job to do. I will conduct a fair enquiry, and your men will be given every opportunity to prove their innocence. But I will not take sides, as I have been appointed to conduct a magisterial enquiry. I hope I have made myself clear?' He nodded and said that he would cooperate fully with the investigation, and that he was sure I would be even-handed in my approach. He stood up, and turning about smartly, disappeared into the darkness outside.

The enquiry progressed fast, with sittings held every alternate day as I, determined to complete the process quickly, turned down requests for adjournments from both sides. Security was tightened at the courthouse where the sittings were held and entry to the courtroom was restricted. And with the CRPF soldiers stopping people at the gate, crowds could be seen standing beyond the fence. Journalists would arrive, sit for a while, conferring with the lawyers and witnesses, take notes and vanish.

The examination and cross-examination of key witnesses took up much of the time. Statements of witnesses was all that one had to go on in such a matter, and it was important to ensure that their testimony was recorded properly so that it could be studied later to see how reliable it was. It was not realistic to expect absolute matching of the testimonies, even with the coaching of witnesses that must undoubtedly have preceded the enquiry. What one could look for was corroboration of the testimony from different sources, like hospital and police records, independent witnesses, and so on. As the enquiry progressed, it became increasingly clear that it was more a matter of whose testimony could be relied on, as those bringing the allegation had one version and the CRPF patrol a completely different one.

The incident was like a hundred other encounters between security forces and the local population, not only in Manipur, but in any 'disturbed' area anywhere in the world. A patrol comes across a group of people who they believe appear engaged in a suspicious activity. They are challenged and stopped and searched. During the search, there is resistance or protest; tempers flare and rough treatment follows. Sometimes this has tragic results with people being killed; in other cases, people are arrested and handed over to the police. Viewed from a distance, it appears reasonable to insist that due process be followed in every such case, with citizens being treated fairly in accordance with the law. But when one has been on patrol for hours and is tired, eyes searching the road ahead for danger, starting at every shadow, suspecting every movement, these niceties can sometimes be forgotten. While following the due process, one can then be quite jumpy and on edge, and can easily react with shocking violence to any perceived threat.

Enquiries conducted in staid courtrooms, with whirring fans and clacking typewriters and paan-chewing clerks with bored expressions, away from the influence of these very real factors of fear and terror and tension and expectancy, can never capture the avalanche-like succession of events that happens in real life that ends in violence and tragedy. It is almost embarrassing to sit there listening to questions fired by complacent lawyers at soldiers and officers about the due process that should have been followed in a search or curfew picket, with the soldier struggling to contain his anger and bewilderment, unable to connect the series of questions with the actual incident that took place in a few minutes amid the hellish din and smoke of gunfire and yells and screams.

I read many reports in mainland newspapers about the excesses of security forces during anti-terrorist combing operations. The general impression conveyed by them was of soldiers running amok, unrestrained by any rules of conduct or code. There was an unstated suggestion that everyone – from the highest-ranking officers to the soldiers – was involved and culpable in this disregard for the rule of law. But what I had seen was very far from this perception. Resorting to gratuitous violence was the exception, not the rule. Officers with a penchant for violent behaviour were marked out and watched carefully by superiors, and were rarely respected by their men. The casualty rate among security forces was higher than it would have been, had there not been sufficient regard for the law and for due process. While soldiers definitely fretted at these restraints, they understood – and their officers constantly reminded them – that they were necessary.

An enquiry such as the one I had been ordered to conduct brought these aspects of the work of security forces into sharp relief. The lawyers, however, appeared blissfully unaware of these realities as they keenly probed the reasons that compelled a soldier to conclude that a person they apprehended had dangerous intentions, and that his moves were calculated to cause harm. The last thing the soldier could offer in his defence was to say that it was dark, and he was tired and jumpy, and that he had been on patrol for the past week, sleeping very little, always on the move, with every movement in the bush or rustle among the leaves being considered a threat.

I wondered at the very small number of violent incidents reported, given the deadly cat-and-mouse game that was played out every hour of every day in many parts of Manipur. After all, this incident had led to a magisterial enquiry being ordered, which meant that it was not a common thing and so had been viewed seriously enough by the powers that be. I wondered why the media never saw things this way, why they took an incident and blew it out of proportion. I realized that to the aggrieved party involved, that was all that mattered. But in all fairness, how long could one go down this road of condemning the security forces without looking at the incident against the backdrop of the task they were given?

After all, it was usually after the politicians had allowed a situation to deteriorate beyond the point where constitutional processes broke down that the security forces were called in to salvage the situation. This aspect was almost wholly forgotten in the clamour for justice and due process that followed.

I remembered a guest lecture at the academy by a retired officer on the subject of civil–military relations. The speaker narrated an incident involving large-scale rioting leading to loss of life and damage to property in Imphal, causing the governor to declare a breakdown of civil administration and handing over the situation to the military. He called the commander of the military garrison and asked him what he proposed to do, to which the army officer replied, 'That is something we will decide after you hand over the situation to us. You people have created the present mess. We will clean it up, but in the way we feel best suits the situation. The army is not the police for you to order about.'

As a rational person, I fully accepted the need for rule of law and due process. But it was only when I donned the hat of a field administrator that I saw that there were situations where extraordinary steps were needed to be taken to restore law and order. There seemed, to my inexperienced perceptions at the time, no way of bridging this divide. Sitting on one side of the divide, there was little possibility of understanding the views of the other side.

Once the sworn affidavits and statements had been checked for signatures and attestations, the documents were neatly bundled and I sat down to write the report. That being completed in a couple of days, I spent a day editing it down to about half its length.

That morning, the CS had called me to enquire about the progress. When I informed him that the report was likely to be ready by that evening, he appeared surprised and asked me whether I was sure I had done a thorough job of it. I assured him that the enquiry had been comprehensive, and he accepted what I said without comment.

That evening, I sat in my office after the others had left, giving the finishing touches to the report. After checking the final draft for typographical errors for the third time, I placed it into a thick envelope. This was sealed and placed into a larger and thicker manila envelope and sealed again. Addressing it to the CS, Government of Manipur, I sat back in my chair, suddenly drained of energy. The telephone rang just then, and I picked it up wondering who could be calling me at that hour in my office.

The familiar voice of the CS crackled through the wires: 'CB, now that you have sealed the cover and only I will open it tomorrow, you can tell me what your finding was!' I stared in amazement at the heavy manila envelope still lying on my desk, wondering at what I had just heard. While I was aware that the DC's office and most sensitive establishments were under constant surveillance of the IB, I did not imagine that this extended to keeping an eye on my comings and goings! I took a deep breath, thought about the CS's words, and deciding that no harm could come of it, replied, 'My finding is that there is insufficient evidence to believe that the alleged atrocity took place.' There was a pause at the other end, and I could hear low voices in the background. Finally he said, 'CB, you have one very happy guy here who will now definitely enjoy the Talisker I have opened for him. For your information, my guest is the director general, CRPF, who arrived this afternoon. I will not invite you to join us because that would be inappropriate. Goodnight. And drop in one of these evenings for a drink. And a game of Scrabble. I must have a return match to avenge that fluke victory you managed to take off me in an unguarded moment!'

I put the receiver down with a smile. A return match would be nice. And the whisky would be excellent too!

Panditji

The light cast by the desk lamp just about lit up a part of the large table piled high with files tagged red in neat stacks. Rows of chairs faded into the gloom where, dimly, a door was framed by the light outside leaking in through a gap in the frame. A green cloth screen hid the wash basin and towel stand. To the other side was the easy chair for the post-lunch nap. A couple of steel cupboards and slotted-angle file racks completed the furniture. The walls were bare but for the mandatory photograph of Gandhi and the two official government calendars, one turned to the following month.

The usual evening sounds of traffic were absent after the imposition of night curfew a few days ago. Though the almost total absence of sound was unusual in any Indian town at any time of the day, I got used to the eerie silence after a few days.

The crunching of tyres on the concrete outside and the clatter of boots rang out in the silence. A curtain parted to allow a glimpse of the visitors. *How did they get past the outer security ring? And why hadn't they been challenged by the guard at the door?* I felt a tightening of the stomach as nameless fears briefly crossed my mind. The door opened and the familiar figure strode in heavily, followed by his gunman who looked around carefully before saluting and withdrawing to his station outside the door.

With a muffled greeting, the man threw his mottled jungle cap on a chair and disappeared behind the screen. The sound of splashing water, followed by the softer slither of soap. Running water again, followed by the rasp of towelling. The man reappeared and sank gladly into the chair after unbuckling his heavy webbing belt and holster, and placing it on the desk.

'Boss, a mug of hot chai will be welcome,' grinned he as he methodically cleaned the automatic, the acrid cordite smell filling the room, surprisingly not unpleasant. The final clicks indicated the ministrations were over and the weapon reloaded. These tasks over, he looked over the desk at me as I sat back quietly, watching him.

'Interesting day, Panditji?' I asked, addressing him by the nickname by which he was universally known, which was an ironic reference to the fact that he was a Brahmin thrust into a warrior's role. Taking a cigarette from the proffered pack, I leaned over to the flaring match held out by him in his cupped hands.

'Uh-huh,' he grunted as he drew on his cigarette and exhaled luxuriously, eyes tracking the plume of smoke as it gushed out. I knew he had something to tell me, and also that he would take his time about it.

'Boss, I was standing at Jain Book Store, keeping an eye on the people passing in the street, when I see this chap wrapped in a shawl come out of the back room and go out. There was something familiar about him and so I decided to follow. My chaps as usual were in plainclothes and covering the street, and we had little difficulty keeping track of him. He stopped at a paan shop and bought something. When he reached under the shawl into his shirt pocket, I caught a glint of light reflecting off something metallic from where I was standing about six feet away. I didn't waste any time and pinned his hands behind his back, while my chaps moved in to cover me. It was all over, and although he struggled and kicked a bit, we didn't have much trouble with him.' Panditji paused to draw another puff from the glowing cigarette. He also appeared to be selecting his words carefully.

'Do you remember Tombi Singh, the young fellow who ran errands at the election department, and who was the life and soul there? And his sudden disappearance? After he left, information about a clever new recruit started to trickle in, a man quite fearless and with a cruel streak, who had started to rise quite rapidly in the ranks of the Mani Singh faction of the People's Liberation Army (PLA). I had my suspicions, but we had nothing concrete to go by. I acted on a hunch and, my friend, sometimes you are saved by those inexplicable things. When we finally caught hold of him, the guy sang like a koel at the interrogation and without losing any time, my team was off to the area near the tourist lodge, where we quickly picked up three key men of the PLA. I must admit I was taken aback when I saw the three sitting quietly in the evening light streaming in through the open windows, looking like friends taking it easy after a hard day's work. Had I made a mistake? Not immediately recognizing me, they seemed relaxed when I went in. But when they finally caught on, they tried to go for their weapons. That was when the rest of the team moved in and we hustled them off quickly before anyone else there knew what was happening. So our friend Tombi had not lied.

'The problem, boss, is that we cannot trust the local cops. Under the law, we have to hand over the fellows we catch to the cops. What almost invariably happens is that in a day or two we are told the men have escaped. Of course the charitable view is that the cops are neither trained nor motivated for handling this task, and that they are probably scared of reprisals; but it is also clear that there are people among them who are willing informers and even possibly members of the underground. So I decided to change my tactics. After we catch a chap, we keep him with us for a day or two, and record the day of arrest as the day on which we hand him over. By that time I have learnt what I want to know, and I don't care if they let the bugger go.

'Sometimes, boss, I know the guy we have caught is a vicious killer who shows no mercy to his victims. Is it not my job to see to it that he pays for his crimes? Better that than having it on my conscience if he is let off and kills again. So you see, my friend, sometimes we have to play God. Or more accurately, cop, prosecutor, judge and executioner, all rolled into one!' There was no amusement in his voice at these remarks.

'And now we come to the strange part of this whole circus. You know how things are with me. I'm in the fight of my life against my own organization to get the promotion I was denied. It has already taken me four years, and cost me a lot in lawyers' fees. If the higher-ups know what I am doing here, they will be the first ones to blow the whistle, not for any love they have for human rights, but just for an opportunity to fix me. It's not easy when you cannot trust your own force. I have to have eyes in the back of my head, boss. Otherwise I would have caught a bullet in my back long ago. Have you watched the movie *Serpico*, released about a couple of years ago? It is about an honest cop who was considered the most dangerous cop by his fellow cops! Because he knew too much. And because he was honest.

'Do you want to know what my real problem is, boss? I know too much. Not about some among the senior officers and their peccadilloes. That's common knowledge, and they don't even bother to hide these things nowadays. These are probably treated as the perks of service in the north-east! I mean I know too much about the underground. This is my second tour of duty here. Since my previous stint in these parts, the PLA has grown into a well-knit formation with a core group of highly motivated fighters. The intelligence services are after the identities of these men. I know every one of the core group by sight, from the time when they were ordinary fellows working in ordinary jobs. I have in my head a file of faces in which they are all there. That's why they carry my picture in their shirt pockets, and why there is a price on my head. If I am killed, with me is lost this file of faces and names. No one else has seen all these guys and can put a name to a face. The PLA guys will never sleep well as long as they know I am on the prowl.

Many of them don't remember my face, and so never know when my hand will fall on their shoulders, like it happened to young Tombi Singh.

'This was not knowledge imparted to me by someone, but something I picked up by keeping my eyes and ears open. I notice things and read every report that crosses my desk, and put two and two together. I therefore am able to see connections that others miss. My driver, orderly, mess boy, and so many others tell me the local gossip, which I filter through the strainer of my knowledge and all these reports. That's why I know so much. They all know that I know. And I know that they know that I know! I have not told my superiors or colleagues about this because I don't trust most of them, and also because in many cases, there are no photographs. Where they are concerned, boss, I am literally the last of the Mohicans. If something happens to me, the pictures of some of the key men in the PLA will go to the flames with me.

'Do you think I will get any medals for what I am doing? You'll be surprised to know that there is not even a citation or commendation for what I have done. Every guy I pick up, every piece of information we extract from an interrogation, is a standing rebuke of the neglect my superiors and colleagues have showered upon me. Not only do I get no thanks, boss, but there are those among my colleagues and superiors who resent and even hate me. Every time I enter the bar at the Officers' Mess, I can sense the conversation die down a bit, and the air getting strained.

'I'm not bitter. This is the way things are. Perhaps I should blame my father for having brought me up with this finely developed sense of right and wrong. Why can't I get on with my life and look after my family while I wait for time to push me up the promotion ladder? Instead of all this risk and danger and sticking my neck out? For what? The dear old country? Yes, sometimes I too am surprised when I realize what that means to me – the uniform, the insignia, the flag. I actually get a lump in my throat that almost suffocates me. And then I don't give a shit for all the danger and hassles I have to go through, because I chose this road of my own free will.

'I feel for my wife, though. Every evening, she dreads the sound of unfamiliar footsteps on the porch, because that may mean that I am not coming back. I think I have an easier time than her, with all that terrible waiting and tension and foreboding. The best part is the way she greets me each time I walk in, like a warrior back from the day's battle. And then I am in heaven, boss. She looks after me till she has to send me off to battle the next day! You know about the time they tried to kill me when she was admitted in the general hospital? They correctly guessed that security would not be easy in the crowded hospital, and that's where they laid a trap for me. I think I know every thought that they think, even as they think it. That's probably why they are so desperate to get me, boss. No disguise will help them if I see them. Unless they see me first!

'So, I had two of my people in hospital gear placed there to look after her. When those who lay in wait for me opened fire, they killed one of the uniformed men but were gunned down by these other two. My wife saw the whole thing from her hospital bed, wrapped in bandages and with an infusion drip line attached to her wrist. The first thing she spoke about when it was over was the family of the officer killed in the incident.

'The funny thing, boss, is that during the ten days she was in the hospital, she did not get any visitors from among the wives of the other officers of my battalion. Their excuse later was that it was dangerous! I've offered to send her to our home town where she will be safe. But she will have none of it. And, boss, deep down I am glad she chose to stay. It would be impossible to take this strain and isolation, day after day, if it were not for the thought that she would be waiting for me when I get back. So your fearsome Panditji, the cold-blooded hunter of terrorists, is actually a softie at heart! Maybe all of us are like this. With another person hidden away inside us.

'Imagine if the insurgents knew this about me? My family will not be safe for a minute, even if I sent them to my home town. They'd find some way of getting to them there. It's better that they believe the other image of me, of an unfeeling and cruel and ruthless man who hunts them down mercilessly. I need all the protection I can get from image and perception, considering I can expect little of that from some of my colleagues.

'You may think I'm getting paranoid, boss. But you will be surprised if I tell you the lengths I go to screen men before I accept them on my commando unit. If I'm alive today, it's because I leave very little to chance, and I suspect every one and every thing. And I have eyes in the back of my head too,' he added with a grin.

'I keep a watch on you, my friend. You are a target because they see you as the guy who issued the curfew orders. An attack on you would be a blow against the state. I know you declined the services of a gunman. That was the right decision because the state police chaps are of little use, with their poor training and antiquated weapons. But you need protection. No one asked me to do this. You are my friend. That's enough reason for me. And I pay my debts. I'll never forget what you did for my men. You are watched by my men at your home, office, and everywhere you go. You won't see them, because they know their work. I'm saying this not to worry you, but just to tell you that you should not assume that the whole machinery of government is there to look after you. You are a good man trying to do a tough job. I like and respect you for that. Therefore, I will see to it that nothing happens to you.'

There was nothing dramatic about the way he said these words, but I was hugely reassured on hearing them. I felt safer that day than I had in a long time. I remember thinking that what others used to put down to my overactive imagination was perhaps not far off the mark. I recalled my imagining getting shot and the obit that would appear in the mainland newspapers. Funny being killed by people whom you felt a sneaking sympathy for, who, despite the tremendous odds, decided to fight against what they saw as injustice against their people. No one anywhere will accept colonial rule, and that basic trait in us humans will always surface when the conditions warrant. As someone said, the Americans should have seen that the Vietnamese people were fiercely independent, and feared and hated China more than they did America. They actually looked to the US to support them in their war of independence against the French. If only the Americans had read history carefully, they would have avoided the frightful mess they got themselves into.

Panditji too seemed lost in his thoughts, looking at the curling smoke from his cigarette. The heavy automatic lay in its leather holster, the belt wrapped neatly around it, both menacing and reassuring.

The Foreigners Are Coming

Life in a field posting in the revenue department is usually enjoyable, and something most young officers look forward to. After all, what can be better than being posted to some far-off district, away from the constant scrutiny of seniors, and being left to one's own devices most of the time. In the district, the best posting was in a subdivision away from the district headquarters. Strong processes and traditions take care of most of the routine work, and the few out of the ordinary events attract the attention of the DC and are usually handled by that worthy, so as not to invite the wrath of the distant state secretariat.

It is only when special activities like elections, the census or natural calamities are visited upon the districts that normal work is thrown out of gear and the smoothly chugging engine of the administration has to move into another gear. These periodic occurrences are viewed by veterans as unpleasant but unavoidable visitations, which have another unpleasant feature that causes stress and heartburn – these activities are not open-ended and almost eternal, like the unending swing between the yin and the yang. They have definite outcomes and deadlines, and failure to meet them can have consequences too terrible to contemplate. Smooth foreheads untroubled by cares crinkle in perplexity when confronted by thick manila envelopes bearing intimidating seals with the words 'ELECTION URGENT' stamped across them in vulgar large print.

While the announcement of an election, be it a by-election or a general one, immediately sets off a series of events that come to a halt only when the process is completed, i.e., once the results are declared and the election return is filed with the Election Commission (EC). However, other activities related to the elections, such as the preparation and revision of the electoral rolls, are more lengthy processes, involving painstaking gathering and verification of information, conducting hearings, weighing arguments, and passing orders. The electoral registration officer (ERO) is the key person in this process, and it is he who determines whether a person's name is to be included in the rolls of a particular constituency. Usually, the SDO is appointed the ERO, and fulfilling the demands of that role takes up most of his attention till the exercise is completed. This responsibility is generally taken up in the run-up to a general election and there is adequate advance notice and also a definite time frame attached to it.

As SDO, Imphal West, I was also ERO for the subdivision, which covered one of the most densely populated parts of Imphal and the Central District, and fourteen Assembly constituencies. The number of voters in the subdivision was large. This was therefore going to be quite a laborious exercise. For the most part, the exercise was well laid out in the manuals, and one had to just follow the instructions. The verification procedure was uncomplicated, except when it came to a dispute regarding a person's normal place of residence, since, in that case, one had to determine where his or her name should be included. Another source of dispute related to students studying in faraway places. If they were to be included, their mailing addresses had to be verified as postal ballots would have to be sent to them. Problems were also likely to arise in the case of persons from other parts of the country temporarily resident in the district, like bank officers, Central government officers, and the like, although in such cases, identity was easily established with certificates from the office of employment.

The usual work of the SDO's office therefore had to accommodate this intrusion, and the office superintendent, usually a senior SDC-grade officer, would resent the claims made by the new work, as well as by the new person who was usually assigned to assist the SDO. Another centre of power that was not answerable to the superintendent was difficult to tolerate but, as the greater experience of the superintendent had taught him, there was nothing to do except endure it. Having to make space for the new arrivals was something everyone hated, as it meant upsetting the finely ordered assignment of space and furniture that had been done carefully in order to reflect the complex pecking order in the SDO's office. If the non-cooperation exceeded limits, it invited actions like arbitrary assignment of space by the SDO. In a couple of cases, this led to the ERO assistants sharing the SDO's room for the duration. Having aliens admitted into the sanctum and tapping away at their typewriters seated opposite the SDO was too much for the veterans to bear, and they would sorrowfully examine their paan before depositing it in a recess under the tongue, and gaze moodily at the coins in their hand to determine the correct change to hand over the panwari.

My work in revising the electoral rolls appeared to be proceeding well, with only a couple of constituencies remaining to be completed. Even among those, most of the tough work in the city wards had been done without a hitch, and all that remained was to complete the work in a few rural areas in the foothills. I reviewed the programme drawn up to complete this work and saw that it involved several trips to outlying panchayat offices where the hearings would be held. While the hill areas had their Hill Development Councils to enable the tribal people to continue with their age-old systems of local government which fitted in nicely with the panchayati raj system favoured by the government, the valley implemented the panchayati raj system in toto. One such inspection was planned at a small settlement in the foothills, where the hills petered out into the vast, absolutely flat plain of the central valley. This panchayat boasted of a mixed population of hill tribals, Meiteis of the valley, and a sprinkling of Biharis, Bengalis, Nepalis and others. While the Meiteis and hill people taken together as a collection of people of local origin dominated, no one group enjoyed overwhelming dominance in numbers, which was one of the stabilizing factors in most districts and villages. A village was referred to as a Naga or Kuki or Mizo village, or as a Meitei village. Other denominations too would live and work there, but there was no doubt about the 'identity' of that village, both to those who inhabited it as well to the outsiders. On this uneasy and apparently unreliable foundation was built the local society and polity.

This settlement presented a challenge to this model, in that a coalition of interests had to emerge in order to fill the vacuum caused by the absence of any one tribe or ethnic group that numerically dominated the others. The tension was testified to by the frequent incidents of violence reported from the village, always involving different tribes or groups. A police outpost stood as the forlorn symbol of the high incidence of disputes and crime, and policemen considered the posting as a punishment for major misdemeanours such as going against the wishes of a minister or influential MLA. If trouble erupted (which was often, judging by the accounts of the locals), the men in khaki fastened the doors, sat around the wireless set and contented themselves by beseeching their superiors to rush assistance to them.

On the appointed day, I arrived at the panchayat office to start the process of conducting hearings for cases where the identity of voters was in dispute. A table and chair had been placed in the meeting room, and several benches arranged in rows. As we settled down, people began to trickle in. Soon, the small 'hall' was full, with people seated everywhere they could find space, including the windowsills. At the appointed time, I called the hearing to order and the process commenced.

Most of the cases were disposed of after a scrutiny of documents. It looked like there were no contentious cases and that we would be able to get through the long list earlier than anticipated. As one more case was cleared and I signed the order in the file, the next case was called.

'Tej Bahadur, son of Ram Bahadur Thapa.'

A young man, neatly attired in jeans and full-sleeved shirt, stood up and shuffled forward. The clerk took the bunch of papers held out by him and after leafing through them, declared that the documents adduced included a ration card, a house tax receipt and a certificate from the school where he had studied. This appeared to be another fit case for inclusion and I was about to pronounce my orders when another man from a group seated on the benches stood up and announced that he objected to the inclusion of Tej Bahadur's name in the rolls. Upon being asked to explain the grounds for objecting, the man said that Tej Bahadur was from Nepal, and that he had entered India illegally and was continuing to live here without valid papers. The objection was recorded and Tej Bahadur was asked to respond to the objection. He again referred to the documents submitted, which clearly proved that he had been a resident of the area for some time. But, as the clerk pointed out, they did not amount to proof that he was a citizen of India.

The case was reserved for orders, as I felt more evidence was needed to arrive at a decision. The next case also involved a person of Nepali extraction, and the same objection was raised, this time by another member of the audience. Again, I had little option but to reserve orders pending production of more evidence. The third case also involved a person of the same origin, with the same result. As more cases were called, and they all met with the same objection, it became evident that what we were dealing with was an organized effort to ensure that Nepalis were not registered in the electoral rolls. The fact that the opposition appeared to be orchestrated did not in itself render the objections invalid. In fact, they appeared to indicate that we were dealing with a problem that was more serious than hitherto suspected. I made a note of it in my diary and decided to meet the DC about it before proceeding with the verification process since it was likely that similar objections would come up in other places too, and there seemed no reason to think that it would be confined to just Nepali immigrants.

On the way back that evening, I pondered about what I had witnessed. Something told me that the issue was not confined to this settlement but would affect Nepalis all over Manipur. The more I thought about it, the more I felt that the electoral registration authorities should study the implications of this happening on a massive scale and report it to the home ministry, both at the Centre as well as in the states. With my vivid imagination and penchant for thinking of worst-case scenarios, I could sense this developing into a huge problem involving hundreds of thousands of people.

The borders of the north-eastern parts of India were porous, with people easily moving across them as a matter of course over many years. These borders often ran along massive rivers and waterbodies, which made marking the exact border a difficult task. When the giant rivers like the Brahmaputra and the Ganga were in spate, they tended to change course, creating new land areas and submerging entire districts, forcing people to shift. This led to seasonal migration of large numbers of people, which was not a problem when the entire area was part of the Bengal Presidency. But after 1947, red lines were drawn over what was topographically, linguistically and culturally one contiguous region, imposing restrictions on the movement of people and their livestock. These lines were swiftly followed by barbed wire and machine gun–toting border guards.

These problems were exacerbated by the economic backwardness of erstwhile East Pakistan (now Bangladesh) as well as Nepal, Sikkim, Bhutan and Burma. So this rich area watered by great rivers became a natural magnet, attracting people in search of a livelihood. Of all these people, the Nepalis were set apart, thanks to their single-minded pursuit of the ambition of any young man in that mountain kingdom: to join the Indian Army, or if that was not possible, to join any other paramilitary force, such as the ITBP, BSF, CRPF, Assam Rifles or Manipur Rifles. In their lexicon, this was called joining the 'battliyan'. Till they achieved this objective, they were willing to work as domestic help, preferably in the homes of government officials who they hoped would be in a position to help them realize their objective.

Back in my quarters, I washed, freshened up and sat down to read the newspapers with a steaming cup of tea brought by the faithful Bal Bahadur. I glanced over the headlines, but my thoughts went back over the day's events. Then I spotted Bal Bahadur reading something with great attention. Upon being asked, he informed me that it was a letter from home. 'No bad news, I hope?' I enquired, to which he replied, 'No, sir. It's from my brother who wants to know when I will join the battliyan.' I then asked him how he got across from Nepal to India, hearing which he began to protest, saying he had lived in India all his life. But I cut him short, saying that I knew better. He then fell silent and, after a pause, went out to his room and returned with a bunch of papers. I glanced through them and found the usual ration card, school certificate and house tax receipt. I then told him about my experience earlier that day, and added, 'Bal Bahadur, if your case came up before me, I'm afraid you'll have trouble proving you are an Indian citizen. So you'd better start thinking about that now, before you are faced with the problem.' To this, he replied quietly, 'I think about it a lot, sir. What other documents can I get?'

I did not have an answer, and I too thought about what his options were. I was brought up short by his next question: 'How will you prove you are an Indian citizen, sir? If you did not have a passport, will you not also produce the same documents that I did? What other proof does a man provide to establish that he is a citizen of India?'

Silence fell as I understood the enormity of the problem we would face if the 'foreigner' issue was exploited by political parties for short-term political benefits.

The Scrutiny of Nominations

I reviewed the arrangements for filing of nominations by candidates for the tenth time, going over each detail with the stoical UDC who was the election clerk. With no change of expression, he started at the top of the page again, going down the long list of items and producing registers or sheets as I called out each item.

Ordinarily, the filing of nominations is not such a complex exercise, with there being no more than a dozen nomination papers to collect, scan, record the oath sworn by the candidate, check the details of those proposing the candidate, check the supporting papers, etc. Nominations are filed at the appointed time and place, and candidates are usually careful to ensure that they are present well before time. Of course, depending on their religious or astrological predilections, the exact time for the filing is often determined by extraterrestrial considerations for some candidates. Even if a candidate makes a mistake, they usually have a backup form along with all necessary certificates, and that can be filed if a major defect is noticed in the first set filed.

In this case, however, what complicated matters was that I, as SDO, Imphal West, was the returning officer (RO) for fourteen Assembly constituencies! This meant that I would have to plan for 140 to 160 nominations to be filed within the stipulated time. Since I could not delegate the task of scrutiny, I had to work out a system that enabled the timely submission of nominations by all candidates, with the scrutiny done by me after they had been checked by the election clerk. This was not easy since the nominations had to be handed over to the RO, and the oath sworn in front of the RO alone. Therefore, a system was devised by the resourceful election clerk, who explained it to me with the air of Einstein explaining a major discovery to a lesser mind. What is more, he always spoke in the royal third person when he spoke in English, which made his words even more delightful.

'Register will be kept outside SDO's room. Manihar will keep register. Candidate will hand over nomination to Manihar, who will enter in register and note time. Manihar will arrange nominations in order of submitting and hand to Tameez Mohammed. After Tameez Mohammed checks nomination, I will hand to SDO-saab (indicating me with an inclination of his head). Candidate will enter SDO-saab's room and swear.'

I suppressed a smile as I imagined having people enter my room, abuse and leave.

'Register will close at five in the evening and Manihar will take it into SDO's room. No more nominations after that,' he added in a tone whose finality was frightening. 'SDO will check all nominations entered in register and accept if in order. No problem,' he concluded modestly.

I listened in admiration to this simple procedure which appeared to have the solution to the problem that had been vexing me. The UDC confirmed that this had been checked with the SDC, Election, in the DC's office, and judging from his expression, if that worthy had cleared the idea, there was no room for any further doubts.

The filing of nominations was to proceed as outlined by the election clerk. The process of checking and accepting nominations including swearing the oath would continue till all the nominations submitted had been cleared. The system appeared foolproof and had been checked with the chief electoral officer (CEO). I congratulated the election clerk for this plan, and he looked pleased at this recognition. I then sat back, happy that one knotty problem had been solved.

The filing of nominations was to commence at three that afternoon, and I was in office an hour before that, seeing to the arrangements. The passage between my office and the courtroom was already beginning to fill up, and the buzz of many voices talking at the same time rose in volume till I had to get the UDC to request the people assembled there to keep it down. This appeared to have some effect, but soon the volume reached and surpassed the earlier level, and I shrugged in defeat and tried to concentrate on the task in hand.

When the hands of the old clock indicated 3 p.m., I gave the UDC the signal to start the process. As he announced that the filing of nominations had commenced, there was a reduction in the noise levels as voices were replaced by the rustling of paper and hushed whispers. Though the procedure was simple and the number of documents to be submitted along with the nomination not too high, the usual nervous repeated flipping through of the papers was very much in evidence as the first candidate shuffled in, along with his proposer. The UDC had already checked the documents, but I went over them again and asked the candidate to repeat the oath and affix his signature. This done, he was requested to leave, which he did reluctantly, casting several glances back at his papers lying on my desk. He was followed by another, and then another, and soon, I was well into the rhythm of the process, which appeared to be going smoothly.

The first to complete the process were almost always the candidates of the major political parties as they arrived with their people, well prepared and briefed about what to do. I saw well-known faces as well: men who had been cabinet ministers in the previous administration. They smiled at me, indicating that they were sure to return, but their confidence was tinged by just that little uncertainty as they espied strong opponents pushing their way through the throng to file their papers. Then there were the

A boy holding a toy gun at a tea shop on the road between Imphal and Bishenpur, 2005

The toy of a child whose father was killed in the violence in the region, 2008

Most Meitei homes have a loin loom in an outhouse; women usually take a few hours off other work each day to weave, Imphal, 2009

1990 LAND RECORD

RIVER NAMBUL 3126

FINE ARTS SCHOOL

KHWAI CREMATION GROUND

FINE ARTS (FRUIT MARKET)

NOW FRUIT MARKET

ANDHI GHAT

C.S.Dag no. 3125

C.S.Dag no. 3119

C.S.Dag no. 3118

C.S.Dag no. 3139

RIPOK SINGDA ROAD

Curious children en route to Ukhrul; in the background can be seen architecture typical of neighbouring state Assam, 1997

A wall painted with municipal land records (years 1960 and 1990)
beside the Nambul river, Imphal, 2005

The view of Imphal, the capital of Manipur, from a nearby hill, 2006

Rice fields ready to harvest take on a golden hue near Imphal, 2003

independent candidates, a diverse group including businessmen, teachers, retired civil servants and others who tried to project a confidence they did not feel. The cheque for Rs 10,000 that they had to deposit would be forfeited if they did not secure more than 10 per cent of the total votes cast, and some of them let go the demand draft for the amount reluctantly, as if wishing to reconsider the whole project of contesting the election. What appeared to be an interesting adventure till a short while ago now seemed to be a futile, quixotic tilting at windmills, a contest they were doomed to lose. A couple of them actually turned around never to be seen again, while others slowly released their grip on the DDs, urged on by those waiting behind them.

The clerk's register slowly started to fill. As the closing deadline approached, a few hurried to get their names entered. Finally, the wall clock chimed to indicate that the appointed hour had arrived. The clerk shut the register with a loud snap, signed at the bottom of the last entry, and took it to the UDC, who checked the last entry and countersigned below the clerk's signature. The nomination papers were bundled securely and brought over to the room where I sat. Those who awaited their turn to complete their nomination formalities waited outside. As their names were called, they entered and took the oath while I quickly checked that their papers were in order. The actual scrutiny would take place in a separate procedure, and conducted as a quasi-judicial proceedings.

Matters appeared to be proceeding without a hitch, and I was beginning to think that it would all be over soon, when everything came to a standstill. The candidate before me was the sitting MLA of a constituency and a minister; he was sure to win this time too. He was a respected senior politician and a familiar figure at the DC's office, which he often visited to take up a grievance on behalf of a constituent. He waited patiently while I scanned the documents, preparing to take the oath when requested to do so. It was then that I noticed that the official letter from his party, nominating him as their candidate, was missing. I looked through the papers again and found it untraceable. I informed the candidate about this, and he was surprised, saying that he was sure he had handed it over to the clerk at the desk. The entry in the register bore out this statement, but the crucial document remained missing. Since the register was the document I relied on to testify to whether the candidate had indeed submitted his papers within the prescribed time limit, I requested him to get a duplicate of the letter and insert it into the set of documents he had submitted.

On hearing this, a man who had been watching this closely from the passage outside my office protested saying that the minister could not be allowed to do this as the deadline had lapsed. Despite me informing him about the reason for my decision, the man continued to protest, raising his voice. I informed him that he could voice his objection at the formal scrutiny of nominations which was to be held later, and that he should allow the process to continue for the time being. This he did with bad grace after he noticed the CRPF men outside begin to move towards the commotion.

It was therefore not a surprise to find later that he was a candidate from that very constituency, representing a militant nationalistic regional party. From his papers, I gathered he was an ex-airman, having been a pilot in the Indian Air Force. He spoke excellent English, was smartly dressed, and I felt spelt trouble with a capital T. I looked through his nomination papers and finding them in order, gestured to him to him to take the oath and sign them. He did so and took the opportunity to voice his strong protest at what he felt was a violation of the electoral rules. I informed him that he could voice his objections during the scrutiny of nominations that was to be held on another day. He looked angry and appeared to be about to launch into another tirade. Then he paused and, gathering his papers and bag, stormed out, muttering under his breath.

The day for the scrutiny dawned bright and clear, and the courtroom was filled with candidates and their agents. The proceedings went smoothly till the contentious nomination papers came up for consideration. I went through the procedure and when I announced that anybody with any objection to the nomination being considered may speak, the pugnacious crew-cut ex-airman stood up and, objected in a loud voice, stating the reasons for his disapproval. I heard him out and ruled that I found the nomination to be in order and complying with the requirements of the electoral rules. He stood there, fury writ all over his face, and with an inarticulate bellow, lunged forward and over the wooden rail separating the presiding officer's desk from the rest of the courtroom, and tried to grab me by the coat. The CRPF jawans who had been prepared for just this contingency swiftly overpowered him and frogmarched him out of the courtroom, shouting expletives and abuse. I sent an official after them with instructions that he was not to be roughed up since he was a candidate, but that he was to be booked if he persisted in creating trouble.

I managed to complete the scrutiny of the remaining nominations without further incident. The courtroom emptied itself and was soon silent again as the staff dispersed for a well-earned lunch, animatedly discussing the morning's incident. I sat in silence, trying to digest the information that had just reached my ears that the troublemaker had made personal threats against me, and that his sympathizers were known supporters of the underground. I was suddenly glad that the CRPF was present, and would be responsible for my safety till the elections were over.

My mind then went over the incidents leading to that day's episode. It was clear that a mistake had been committed by someone, but the real problem was that there was no clarity about what I was to do in the circumstances. The rule was simple: no nominations were to be accepted after the deadline had passed. But what was to be done in a case where there is evidence that the nomination had been received within the stipulated time, but was subsequently misplaced? I did the only thing I felt I could do, and that was to get the candidate to fill out another nomination form. Technically, it was done after the deadline had passed. But I believed I had observed the spirit if not the letter of the law.

As I thought more about the matter, I began to suspect that there was more to the incident than met the eye. Was the other candidate who objected somehow involved in the disappearance of the original nomination form? The missing papers were those of the sitting MLA and rival of this ex-airman, whose chances against the incumbent were not good, given his party's standing and his personal record for rude and abrasive behaviour. With the sitting MLA out of the way, the chances of this candidate winning became considerably brighter. If the papers were removed, he had to have an accomplice in my office. I ruled out my diligent election clerk but had some suspects from among the rest of them.

What was I to do about these suspicions? I could report the matter to the CEO of the state, which would no doubt be forwarded to the EC. There would follow enquiries and reports and the file would grow fatter as correspondence between Delhi and Imphal progressed. The elections would come and go and the sitting MLA would probably get re-elected. The aggrieved candidate would file a petition which would take note of the fact that the matter was being looked into by the EC. It was clear that no useful purpose would be served by this course of action.

Taking a decision based on my reading of the facts and handling the direct consequences appeared to be the best idea. I believed I was acting in the best interests of the electoral process as well as the rules. There are many instances when the action to be taken appears to be simple, based on the rules applicable. But peculiar circumstances make it less easy to view it in such a simple fashion. This is especially true of law and order situations when it becomes difficult, if not impossible, to comply with what appears to be the law, in a situation where the exigencies of the real situation cannot be properly recreated or explained. That is why many enquiry commissions appointed to look into actions involving the use of force do an injustice to those who had to handle the situation as it developed on the ground. The same appeared to be the case in the present situation. I was clear in my mind that I had done the right thing and decided to stick to my decision. Trying to play it safe and merely reporting the matter would have compromised the process of election that had been set in motion.

It is this fine distinction between doing the right thing and doing things right that often needs to be faced by a government official without the advantage of reference to higher authority or clarity from a manual or handbook. To understand this better, one needs to look at the role of a referee in a game of football. A punctilious application of the rules of football can reduce a game to an endless series of violations of various kinds. No rhythm or movement can ever develop in the game if such an approach is adopted. Each half will be punctuated by a constant series of violations and infringements, with play being stopped every few seconds. A good referee knows when to intervene and when to allow the game to go on. Enjoying a good game and *not* applying the rules of the game is the real objective, with the better team winning the contest.

A nuanced approach to the application of rules is necessary so as to ensure that violations are not permitted but we are able to rectify mistakes swiftly, without allowing technicalities to stand in the way of justice and reasonableness. In real life, there are many situations that call for speed and decisiveness, where much is at stake and no time ought to be lost to indecisiveness or an excessively bureaucratic approach. It is amusing that the training imparted at the academy does not stress such cases, and therefore each young officer has to rely on experience or a mentor to guide him or her when such situations actually develop.

The Countermanded Election

I checked off the long list running down the page. The pencil in my hand had marked each item as I looked at the file on the desk. I could not afford to make a mistake as that would render the election results of that constituency void, necessitating a re-poll. I was sure that that was the most common nightmare of all election ROs, which was probably why most ROs slept with the blue RO's handbook wedged under their pillows.

There were many details that had to be checked, being careless about any one of which could lead to a fatal flaw in the whole electoral process. The handbook was a marvellous document that enabled even a rookie to conduct an election successfully as long as he ensured that he had followed instructions to the letter. Of course it helped if you had staff trained in election matters and already familiar with the processes involved. When your election staff consisted of a UDC who was the only one in the office who spoke barely adequate English, you realized your resources were thin. And when the process had to be repeated with the same care for another thirteen constituencies, you knew you were up against it.

Obviously, the powers that be placed great faith on the almost magical qualities of the handbook, because the training was quite perfunctory and comprised several chatty briefings to all the ROs of the state by the CEO and his team. This was completed in less than a day, and all of us present were cheerily told that all we had to do was follow the handbook carefully and there would be no problem. There was only a brief mention of the fact that even a minor deviation from prescribed procedure could place the entire election process at risk. That it would be a black mark and would inflict a fatal wound on one's Confidential Record, that most sacred of all records, which would haunt one till the day one retired.

While the DC, as the district electoral officer, was nominally in charge of the electoral process in the district and performed a coordinating role, he did not have statutory powers over the ROs, who reported directly to the EC for all matters relating to the electoral process. All reports had to be sent directly to Delhi in thick envelopes under special certificate of posting with the words ELECTION URGENT stamped prominently across the front. My jeep now sported, in addition to the usual 'SDO, Imphal West' board, another sticker that read ELECTION URGENT in red. It was not clear what additional privilege this sign secured, but soon there were many vehicles sporting these signs whizzing importantly about the town and valley.

For the month before the actual polling day, all other activity at the SDO's office came to a crawl as election-related work pushed all else aside. Even the lexicon of the place changed with the usual terms elbowed aside in favour of new phrases such as RO, CEO, DEO, handbook, EC, candidate, polling agents, polling officers, etc. Given the limited resources at my disposal, I had to rely almost entirely on the UDC and myself to complete the many electoral processes without error or omission. This again meant that the two of us spent most of our time closeted in my spacious office room, with the stenographer occasionally in attendance, working our way laboriously through the long checklist. The rest of the staff members helpfully looked in periodically, their concern writ large on their frank open faces, with little to offer by way of assistance.

The UDC was a burly man with a balding head, always impeccably turned out in well-matched trousers and coat, with a shirt open at the collar and a woollen muffler wrapped around his throat. Clean-shaven and on the dark side, his was a reassuring presence during these strain-filled days as one by one, the various deadlines approached and passed. He always arrived before time, and was ready to start work with all the necessary files and papers spread out on the large table. The two of us sat across each other, the better to be able to confer and refer to files and registers. The only recesses he permitted himself were the fairly frequent visits to the lavatory and the equally frequent couple of minutes he took to roll and tuck into a corner of his mouth another paan from a little silver box he carried in his capacious coat pocket. This often meant that the first few words he uttered after such a 'paan break' were little more than liquid gurgles which gradually formed themselves into words one could comprehend.

And so the days ground by, slowly and painstakingly, as we hunched over the large table covered with files – some fully exposed, some kept open with the assistance of other files, some flagged with colourful strips of paper marked with inscrutable notings that only the UDC could decipher. The office lambu who normally went about his work of dispensing mugs of tea, cheerfully unaware and unconcerned about what was going on in a particular room, now appeared to tiptoe around when he entered the room, and spoke only in a theatrical hushed whisper. This phenomenon appeared to afflict all the staff of the office, and I suspect it had something to do with the fact that no one was really aware of what was going on but they realized that something important was monopolizing our attention.

In the office hierarchy, the UDC was not the natural Number 2. That was the elegant Ibobi Singh who enjoyed the rank of SDC and was the office superintendent. Impeccably attired in a suit every day of the week, he was a picture of sartorial correctness, with no crease or fold marring the dignified picture he cut as he stepped off the rickshaw that brought him to office each day. His rimless spectacles perched on his slender nose, his clean-shaven face, high forehead, carefully combed brilliantined grey hair, his hands with the many rings on various fingers and his shining shoes, all bespoke the 'gentleman' that Ibobi Singh was to his very core.

Such seemed his sense of correctness that he did not seem to see anything amiss in the SDO being closeted with a mere UDC while he, occupying the superior grade of SDC, sat quietly in his room with not a single summons to the SDO's office throughout the day. Ibobi Singh's cool manner suggested he was sufficiently experienced in the ways of government to know that once every so often, the natural order of things in the government suffered an upheaval due to the elections, census, riots, disasters, floods, and other such acts of God, which meant new ways of workflow appearing temporarily. Ibobi Singh sported a tolerant, benign smile that suggested he knew that these seemingly cataclysmic changes were mere temporary disturbances, and that he was certain of the ultimate triumph of the order he loved and upheld so zealously. Hushed whispers in the corridors praised Ibobi Singh for facing these trying times like a gentleman since he knew that the day was not far off when the UDC – who played snakes and ladders with the natural order and hobnobbed with the SDO today – would have to bow to the old order and await the peremptory summons of the bell on Ibobi Singh's desk.

However, I knew that despite his outward calm demeanour, Ibobi Singh was suffering agonies inside at this seeming neglect. But I also knew that he was of little help during the elections, and that the DC was correct in his assessment of the capabilities of the staff – that the UDC was the only one who could be relied on to do a good job when it involved meticulous attention to detail. And so I had to act as if I did not notice little things like Ibobi Singh walking gravely past us, opening an almirah, picking up and soon replacing a file or two, shutting the almirah door gently, and retreating the way he came. The stiff back and stately gait seemed to reproach me for my neglect of this fine man. But I had enough on my plate without having to worry about Ibobi Singh's sensibilities.

As each day passed, one more set of activities to be completed was checked off by the diligent UDC. Like a prisoner crossing off each day spent in his cell to contemplate the remaining days of his servitude, I considered the days that remained to be free of this wearisome responsibility. Not being comfortable with detail at the best of times, what made the process even more irksome was the compulsive need to go step by step, without any possibility whatsoever of 'skipping' a few innocuous-looking steps. This painstaking plodding from one step to the next made an already onerous process even more of a burden. My marked lack of enthusiasm for the task must have been obvious to all but the most unobservant eye.

And so the tasks were completed in what seemed to be slow motion: the filing and scrutiny of nominations, training of polling staff, inspection of the polling stations, checking the equipment of each team of polling staff, arranging their transport and security, having standby resources in case people reported sick (which was a common ruse to get out of polling work), sending people over to verify whether the person was actually ill, and so on in interminable and mind-numbing detail. All this was to be accomplished with the assistance of just the UDC, and repeated thirteen times more every day. Every evening, I left exhausted, convinced that I had forgotten things that would render null and void the elections to at least three important constituencies.

As matters wore on to their remorseless and preordained conclusion of a hopefully duly conducted and concluded poll, I began to think that things may not go terribly wrong after all, that perhaps I was overestimating the complexity of the task, and also underestimating the resourcefulness of the UDC. Then the telephone rang one evening and I was informed that a candidate, Thokchom (Th.) Bira, had been shot and had been admitted in a serious condition in the Medical College Hospital. While Rajen

Singh was summoned from his home, I hastily threw on some warm clothes and sat leafing through the handbook, trying to see what it had to say about such a contingency. It had much to say, since the death of a candidate was a serious matter that had to be regarded as an event that materially affected the election to the candidate's constituency. This meant that the election had to be cancelled or 'countermanded', as the handbook primly held, by the EC, based on the report by the RO confirming the death of the candidate. Rajen Singh soon arrived, not amused at this call at what was obviously a very inconvenient time, and we were soon careening about dangerously on our way to the hospital.

Once there, the familiar unpleasant smells of a large Indian hospital took over. I have always felt queasy when entering a hospital, and had to take a deep breath before stepping in, almost as if I wanted my lungs to manage the whole hospital visit with what I sucked in that single breath. The policemen on duty took me quickly across to the casualty ward. There, the bed in the corner with the still figure covered with a sheet told the story that the candidate was dead. Even so, the rules required that I see the body and the death certificate, and thereby satisfy myself that the candidate was truly dead, before reporting the fact to the EC. He had been shot through the head, the bullet entering at his left temple, and exiting through a large hole behind his right ear, in the process having removed most of his brain it encountered on its passage through. These necessary steps were duly carried out by me, and soon I was heading for the General Post Office (GPO) to send off the priority teleprinter message to the EC. That done, I waited for the acknowledgement from the EC. That arrived soon, and I walked out wearily to where Rajen Singh, his good humour now restored, was regaling an attentive audience of several pretty but tired and sleepy-looking nurses with what was obviously a gripping anecdote.

Seeing me, he brought the jeep round to the front and we set off. On the way back, I thought of the candidate who had just become another grim statistic in the EC's annals, someone whose death had led to the countermanding of a poll. Th. Bira was a much respected member of the recently dissolved assembly, the lone member of the Communist Party in the house, respected by his people, and known for his honesty and uprightness. The identity of the killers was not clear, although the police would be quick to lay the blame at the door of the insurgents. I had met Th. Bira several times, and found him a good-humoured and educated man, always well attired in a conservative suit or odd coat, without a tie, but with a thick woollen scarf wrapped round his throat, and a Nepali-looking cap on his head. That picture alternated with another, of a still figure on a hospital bed covered in a white sheet in a corner of a large ward. The image slowly faded from my memory, waves of sleep pouring over me. I was soon nodding off to sleep, despite the jeep swaying from side to side, with Rajen Singh anxious to deposit me back home before making his way back to his.

The Elopement Season

It was already dark when I stepped out of the jeep at my quarters. Rajen Singh parked the vehicle and, handing over the keys, climbed on to his bicycle and pedalled off down the lane, chewing on the paan he had inserted into his mouth a short while earlier, and humming some popular ditty.

The door opened and I was relieved of the briefcase and files by Bal Bahadur. I thanked my stars for getting him as my help as he was the envy of all my colleagues who visited me. The quarters were spotlessly clean, with everything in its place at all times. Clothes were always folded and put away, the floors were clean and wiped, the tables and shelves dusted. The kitchen was the pièce de résistance, with the few utensils gleaming in neat rows, arranged by size. Spoons of assorted sizes and shapes sprouted from a wide-necked jar meant for some other purpose, but now looked like a bunch of flowers in stainless steel!

In my bedroom, I removed my dusty footwear and put on the slippers that had been placed next to my chair. After freshening up, I returned to the drawing room and sat in my favourite cane chair, newspaper open. A mug of piping hot tea was already on the side table, and I sipped the excellent tea in silent appreciation as my eyes glanced over the headlines. The newspaper was published from Kolkata and came by the Indian Airlines flight via Guwahati, and so I got to read it only in the evening. The happenings in

India (even I had begun to say that, I thought wryly!) seemed very far away. I noted the almost total absence of news from the southern part of the country and turned to the sports page to see whether anything interesting had happened on the cricket scene. The Ranji matches were in progress and the selectors were on the prowl, looking for new faces to include in the team to meet the visiting West Indian cricket team. I wondered about the prospects of a new young pace bowler who was beginning to wreak havoc in Haryana.

The peremptory ring of the telephone interrupted this pleasant line of speculation. It was a fellow officer, excitedly relaying the news that another colleague had been arrested for being an accessory to an elopement. This was too much to digest over a telephone call, and I thought it over as I pulled on a pair of shoes and brushed my hair to wait for the colleague to arrive.

The sounds of a vehicle pulling into the drive were followed by several pairs of feet hurrying up the short path to the door. Soon, the tiny room was filled with four others, all speaking simultaneously. I was able to piece together the facts of the case: a girl had eloped with her paramour, and an IAS officer had been arrested for aiding and abetting the act. The girl being a Meitei and the paramour being a Mizo complicated matters. Adding fuel to this already incendiary mixture was the fact that the alleged co-conspirator was also a Mizo, and an IAS officer holding a responsible position in the secretariat.

Elopements were common in Manipur, especially in the valley dominated by the Meitei community. Unlike the hill tribes in which young men and women could mix freely, the situation was quite different among the Meiteis. Their culture was heavily influenced by two quite diverse forces. One was the indigenous set of beliefs that constituted Meitei culture, which was quite distinct from the way of life of the hill tribes. This was rooted in the settled agriculture and occupations that sprang up in the valley dominated by the Meiteis. They were ruled by a monarchy and had developed customs and practices similar to small princely states that managed to carve out an independent existence even during the British colonial period. It was only when the British moved into the hill areas of what was then called Assam that Manipur too came under British rule.

The other major influence was Hinduism. Manipur represents probably the only case of aggressive Hindu proselytization, which happened when the royal family of Manipur embraced Vaishnavaite Hinduism and decided to impose its choice on the rest of the populace. Vaishnavaite preachers were imported from Orissa to carry out the task of conversion and a proud people who had held their own against both the Ahom kings as well as the Arakan kingdom found themselves embracing a faith that was alien to them. What was more remarkable was the thoroughness with which the social baggage of Hindu society, especially the caste system, was also transplanted to unfamiliar ground. A people who did not have any form of social discrimination other than the feudal relations that usually characterize agrarian societies ruled by monarchies found themselves having, literally overnight, a fully developed caste system superimposed on their social structures. It only remained to fix the various social groups in to the chaturvarna hierarchy. This was done with amazing thoroughness. At the top were the Brahmins with the caste surname Sharma, then the Kshatriyas with the surname Singh, and then various groups which were classified into Sudra and even untouchables. All the absurd practices associated with caste 'pollution' made their appearance in this tiny valley, thousands of miles from Kerala, where Vivekananda, when confronted with the concepts of distance pollution and other extreme phenomena related to the caste system, declared Kerala to be a 'madhouse'. Since Hinduism has been famously described as more a way of life than a religion, what happened in effect was the near obliteration of another way of life that had existed for hundreds and possibly even thousands of years.

Meitei extremism was a late starter in the north-east, preceded by vigorous opposition to the Indian Union by the Nagas and Mizos. My guess is that initially the Meiteis did not want to be seen as making common cause with the hill tribes who were once their subjects, and whom they regarded as inferior. While the hills embraced Christianity with enthusiasm, wanting to share in the benefits of education and identity that came with it, the Meiteis held back, regarding their Hindu heritage as equal to if not superior to the Christian one. In the early years of the young Indian nation, as social groups jockeyed and bargained for a place in the sun and extracted important concessions, including reservations for scheduled castes and tribes, the Meiteis, not wishing to be bracketed with their erstwhile subjects and vassals, refused to be categorized as backward, therefore missing out on important reservation privileges. This led to the almost total absence of Meiteis in the upper echelons of the administration, while their counterparts from among the Nagas and the Mizos were recruited into these prestigious services and came to occupy high positions in the region, including Manipur.

Coming back to the case in hand, a police complaint had been filed by the girl's father, naming the IAS officer as an accessory after the fact. The local police officer, also a Meitei, had acted with unusual alacrity and arrested the officer at his residence, and had clapped him in the lock-up for the night. It was unusual for an IAS officer to be arrested for any charge ordinarily, and for one to be arrested for such a reason clearly meant there was more to the case than met the eye. Enmities between tribes and communities simmer just below the surface in the north-east, and the law and order establishment has to be unusually sensitive to these factors in those parts. A simple street altercation can explode with shocking suddenness into a riot, causing loss of life and destruction of property. The present situation appeared to be ripe for such a denouement unless nipped in the bud. It was going to be a long night.

The police station was tense, with edgy policemen, mostly Meiteis, nervously fingering their weapons and huddling in clusters. News had come of groups of Mizo youths assembling at a few places, with wild talk of storming the police lock-up and releasing the arrested officer. The police station appeared to be wholly incapable of repelling a determined assault and I thought that it would be better to be elsewhere when the assault actually took place! I spoke with my counterpart in the police and advised him to come over to the police station to try and defuse the situation. The subdivisional police officer (SDPO), being a mayang, would be able to act in a way no local could.

The girl's father, accompanied by kinsmen, was standing to one side, with everybody in his group talking with raised voices. They were soon joined by the MLA of the constituency who proceeded to make a wholly inappropriate speech calculated to whip up passions further. I sent word to the MLA to come over to where we were standing and advised him to soothe frayed tempers instead. My companions then entered the station to talk to the hapless arrested officer and found him dispirited and low, sitting on the floor in a dirty cell, clad only in his vest and underwear. Although not beaten, he had obviously been handled quite roughly. He burst into tears on seeing his colleagues, but was also clearly relieved.

Efforts were under way to secure his release, but we were not making much progress, with everyone trying to get someone else to take the decision. Finally, the matter reached the IGP and the CS, both of whom were not amused at being disturbed late in the evening for such a matter. By then, however, emotions were running high, and both realized they would have to act swiftly to defuse the situation before it turned ugly, not just between the Meiteis and the Mizos but between the IAS and the police too. While parleys were in progress at the highest levels, an emergency meeting of the IAS Association was called, and members started arriving at the Officers' Club.

When at last the meeting was called to order, the matter was presented by the aggrieved officer's friend and fellow Mizo. The presentation was emotional, and painted a picture of an innocent officer wrongfully arrested just to satisfy the vengeful wishes of the Meitei community which could not tolerate one of its girls eloping with a Mizo. An animated discussion followed, with everything from the unity and integrity of the country to standards of civilized behaviour being invoked. Meanwhile, the news from the discussion between the CS and IGP was not good, with both worthies apparently choosing to go with the time-honoured strategy of doing nothing in tricky situations.

The discussion at the special session of the IAS Association was getting increasingly animated. A senior officer took the floor and broke into a paean of praise for the CS and his sagacity and wisdom, on which qualities he expounded at length, to the bewilderment of those present. He wound up by proposing that a formal resolution be moved to thank the CS for his exemplary initiative to resolve the problem.

Unable to contain his anger any longer, an elderly officer who had been silent thus far and contenting himself by chain-smoking in a corner thumped the table loudly and raised his voice: 'I cannot believe my ears. A fellow officer has been arrested and thrown into the lock-up on a flimsy unsubstantiated charge and what do we fellow officers do? We babble on about what a great job the CS is doing, when actually nothing at all has been done! When a similar incident happened in Bihar a few years ago, the CS and his senior colleagues met the CM and informed him that they would tender their resignations unless the guilty policemen were punished. And here we have a useless debate going on! If I stay here any longer, I will puke.' With these words, he pushed his chair back and stalked out of the room.

An awkward silence fell, and several moments passed with no one moving a finger. Finally, someone fidgeted, a chair scraped back, feet shuffled here and there, low voices muttered in the background, and signs of life returned to the group. Faint protests at the violence of the honourable gentleman's accusations began to be heard and started gaining in volume.

Just then, someone dashed in and whispered something to the president of the association. He listened, cursorily at first, then with much more attention as the import of the message sank in. With an expression of relief, he rose and pounded the table to get everybody's attention. When some order had returned to the room, he announced that the problem had been resolved and that the fellow officer had been released from police custody; that the charges had been withdrawn and, in a manner of speaking, all's well that ends well. The announcement was greeted with enthusiasm and someone shouted: 'Three cheers for the CS and the IGP. Hip hip hurraaaah!'

The company began to disperse, with small groups lingering, some discussing the events, others talking knowledgably of the brilliance of the CS, yet others referring to the cunning of the IGP which must surely have been behind the resolution of the issue. Then there were others who were disappointed at the promising situation being abruptly brought to a close. Each group warmed to its topic and started for the door, obviously headed for the Officers' Club bar to pursue more spirited discussions.

Therefore, they missed the dry, laconic announcement by a junior officer who informed the few who remained that the girl had returned home on finding that the 'Mizo' boy was actually a Meitei who was already married, that her parents learnt that the actual culprit who encouraged her was her maternal uncle who harboured a grudge against her father, that the uncle had been beaten severely by the father with the assistance of several bystanders as well as the police who felt badly used in the whole affair, and that the discussion between the CS and IGP was continuing at the former's residence.

The young courier looked around him to observe the effect of his words, and finding little response, grinned and left the club, passing the other groups that were continuing to pursue their theories which were beginning to take on the proportions of epic sagas of cunning and deceit. *One more legend to add to the many already floating around in the misty valleys and hills of Manipur,* I thought as I moved aside to let a shapely young Meitei lass sashay past in her fitting white blouse and tightly wound sarong. *I wouldn't mind eloping with that one,* I thought as she brushed past with a sidelong glance, a smile hovering on her full lips.

I climbed into the jeep, and pulling my jacket tight around myself and raising my collar to ward off the chilly wind, drove off into the night.

Picketing the Raj Bhavan

It was early afternoon, with the winter sun high but at an angle, the light slanting in through the office windows. I sat dictating final orders in a land dispute case. Opposite me, the steno was hunched over his work. This was slow work, with many clarifications sought in every sentence during the dictation. It was obvious that many of the words were new to him, and he was transcribing the sounds he heard as best as he could. For all the progress we appeared to be making, I could very well have written the orders out in long hand for them to be typed later. I sighed and paused yet again while the steno peered at his notes and asked me to repeat the previous sentence. My eyes rising heavenwards in exasperation, they encountered the smiling portrait of the Father of the Nation on the far wall. Even he could see the humour in the situation.

The telephone rang; it was the DC asking me to proceed urgently to the Raj Bhavan gates where a picket line of protesters had formed. The governor was due to arrive later that afternoon, and the DC wanted the road cleared before that. I hurried out asking Rajen Singh to bring the jeep to the porch, and went straight to the ADM's office. Barging in without ceremony, I found myself interrupting a discussion between the ADM and three others. The former looked up and seeing it was me, broke into a grin and asked me to sit and have a paan. I declined, explaining why I was in a hurry, and requested him to requisition a posse of policemen to handle any contingencies. I specifically asked for a platoon with a few women constables, as the picketing agitators were schoolteachers protesting about something, and there were bound to be several women among them. I recalled several embarrassing situations on earlier occasions when we had been confronted by agitators who were mostly women and not one woman constable among our number.

As I hurried out to the waiting jeep, I heard the ADM's parting shot regarding his offer of assistance in case I found the female teachers too hot to handle. I grinned thinking of the ADM with his rangy good looks that had all the women in the DC's office sighing as he went past. Despite his ladykiller reputation, he was basically a light-hearted chap who did not take himself and his job too seriously and as a result was a very good companion – entertaining and amusing. I enjoyed his company and looked forward to the evenings when we met either at his place or mine over a bottle of rum, enjoying the banter or the occasional game of Scrabble or cards.

As the jeep swerved through traffic and narrow streets with Rajen Singh using his superior knowledge of the town to get us to the Raj Bhavan gates in the shortest possible time, I went through the checklist of things that needed to be done in such situations: police force that included women constables, a lathi contingent, a few armed constables, a couple of trucks to remove the arrested protesters, 'magistrate' badges (there had been instances of magistrates getting beaten in lathi charges as policemen failed to distinguish between the young chap in civilian clothes and the protesters in the melee!); police officers with walkie-talkies; ascertaining the location of DC and ADM, etc. Everything seemed to be in order, or so I thought as the jeep turned into the broad avenue running along the bund. The Raj Bhavan compound ran along one side of the road. On the other side glistened the still waters of the Kanglaipak bund – a moat that surrounded the old Kangla Fort in the heart of Imphal. The jeep screeched to a halt, wheeling across the road as it did so, right in front of the imposing gates of the Raj Bhavan with its huge brass Ashoka lions and emblem on the pillars on either side.

Three police vans were already at the gates. *Good! That part taken care of.* The officer sat in his jeep, watching as my vehicle approached. *Odd, his continuing to sit as I climb out.* Ordinarily, the police chaps were quite deferential where IAS officers were involved. As I approached, the officer got out with deliberate slowness and stood in all his uniformed magnificence. It was none other than Manihar Singh, the pride of Manipur Police, with his drop-dead good looks and sartorial elegance. With every turn, polished brass emblems and insignia flashed and glittered. *I must be looking like the janitor,* I thought sourly as I approached the magnificent figure striking a pose, silver-tipped stick tapping against razor sharp trouser crease.

'Good morning,' I said with a smile. He loftily acknowledged the greeting with a slight inclination of the head, turning to show me his left profile which was no doubt the one he personally preferred. I self-consciously tried to shoot my shirt cuffs that had retreated into my coat sleeve, only to discover they were rumpled, and so quickly pushed them back inside. A surreptitious rub of the shoes against the trouser leg failed to bring a shine to shoes that, despite Bal Bahadur's ministrations, could not conceal the fact they had seen better days. *What the hell am I doing, trying to compete with this puffed-up dandy,* I thought with some irritation. *I'd better review the arrangements and see how the situation is developing.*

All this posturing because the rule book was not clear about the hierarchy, especially about where an SDO stood vis-à-vis an ACP. This was a running problem the IAS had with the IPS, especially in field situations, and one that had to be handled with 'tact and firmness' – a phrase that was thrown around by administrators long in the tooth, but to practise which was never taught in the academy!

The ACP noted with satisfaction my dishevelled and rather tacky appearance, then adjusted his peak cap a bit, smartly rapped his trouser leg with the brass-studded cane he held, and overall gave the appearance of a man accustomed to having the situation under control. On my asking how many policemen he had with him, he barked an order to a subordinate and stood negligently by, examining well-manicured fingernails as the other lower functionary answered that there were two sections of armed police ready in the vans. When I enquired about the women constables and the lathi police, I received blank stares in reply. With rising irritation, I pointed out that there were several hundred schoolteachers blocking the road, that the governor was due to arrive in a couple of hours, and that we may have to use force to clear the road. My enquiring sarcastically if the plan was to open fire on the demonstrators to clear the road brought home rather crudely the situation we were in. There was not enough time to get the appropriate reinforcements and it looked as if we would have to make do with what resources we had.

A brief look at the strutting ACP conjured up visions of the latter whipping out his gleaming pistol from the shiny hew holster and loosing off a few rounds at the yelling teachers, while his men formed neat ranks like the musketeers of old in the period war movies, methodically loading, aiming and firing at the commands issuing from their officer, and then calmly reloading while the row behind levelled their weapons and fired. I could see scores of people fall in the hail of gunfire, writhing and thrashing on the ground, with the ACP urging his men on to more mayhem and slaughter. Blaring newspaper headlines rose before my fevered eyes: SLAUGHTER AT RAJ BHAVAN GATE. SDO ORDERS BLOODIEST POLICE FIRING SINCE JALLIANWALA BAGH!

While the ACP perhaps did not have as vivid an imagination as me, he too must have seen the ugly possibilities that could stem from his oversight. But he appeared bereft of ideas and contented himself with examining the threadwork in his peak cap. The situation appeared to be moving towards something bad if not exactly the terrible denouement foreseen by me, and there seemed little I could do to prevent the inevitable. I think it is almost always a combination of trivial, innocuous things that results in an explosive cocktail. A crowd of agitating teachers on an empty stretch of broad road in broad daylight does not represent the makings of a tragedy. The fact that the governor was due to pass that way in a few minutes introduced the fatal seasoning to complete the mixture, transforming it into an incendiary one.

There I was, along with a posse of armed policemen, charged with the task of clearing the road before the motorcade arrived. The agitating teachers didn't know that, and probably planned to disperse in a couple of hours. As the minutes ticked by, I started to feel the pressure build up in me and found myself looking at my watch every few seconds, a sure sign that my mind was beginning to feel the strain.

The policemen lounged unconcernedly as they were unaware of the approaching motorcade. *Should I ask them to leave their weapons in the van and move on the agitators unarmed? If I do so, will they obey my instructions?* The ACP was still lost in contemplation of the fate line on his palm. What was I to do? *What if,* I thought wildly, the agitators were still there when the motorcade arrived? There will be a hold up, that's all! *But things can go terribly wrong,* I thought again. What if the motorcade tried to force its way through? And some of them attacked the vehicles? And the governor got trapped in the melee? This was not a promising line of thought, and I resolved to stop my habit of imagining the worst-case scenarios, an amusing habit I had honed while participating in group discussions at the academy.

Then my eyes fell on an elderly head constable standing by one of the police vans, his jaws moving rhythmically as he, like many others, chewed a mouthful of paan contemplatively. He appeared to be trying inconspicuously to attract my attention. I called him over to where we were and asked him to tell us what he had to say. The ACP stood stiffly in perplexed magnificence, wondering whether he should allow this bypassing of his authority, and then deciding that prudence was the better part of organizational hierarchic propriety, looked out intently at the shouting and gesticulating crowd as if trying to decide a suitable punishment for its transgressions.

The head constable, having expectorated a long stream of paan juice expertly across the road, calmly suggested that the armed policemen would leave their weapons with the safety catches on. There would be no bullet in the breech; he would personally see to that too. They would then hold the weapons across their chests and be prepared to wield them as clubs if necessary. Announcements would be made by him in suitably blood-curdling words and tone about the terrible consequences that awaited the picketing teachers if they did not disperse. The men would then advance in a solid line right at the centre of the picket line, which should break. 'What if it doesn't,' I asked, having visions of policemen clubbing teachers with rifle butts. The head constable shrugged and stolidly repeated that the line would break.

I went over the proposal and decided that it was the only idea worth pursuing if the picket line had to be cleared before the motorcade arrived. It had to be ensured that every single weapon's safety catch was actually on, as otherwise we could have a terrible accident. I considered various scenarios, some of them quite improbable, which gave me something to do while the head constable went down the ranks of the policemen, checking whether they had put their safety catches on. My assiduous sifting of possibilities finally came up with a problem: what if there were many women in the front row and they refused to move as the police line approached? Could we have the men push their way through? What would happen if a policeman clubbed a woman protester with the butt of his rifle? Definitely not a nice scenario to consider, and one that I tried to dismiss. I peered at the distant picket line through the light which had steadily got worse over the past half-hour, trying to see whether I could spot the women. But from that distance, it was impossible to distinguish between the figures, most of whom seemed to be wearing trousers and thick jackets or parkas.

Feeling more on edge with all the waiting, I walked over to where the head constable was checking the final weapon. He appeared satisfied with his arrangements. However, I noticed that he kept glancing at his watch and then at the sky overhead, and wondered why. Was the motorcade early? Had the governor decided to arrive by helicopter? I asked the head constable to find out from the impressive ACP, who had by now polished his belt buckle with a kerchief and was trying to check the results of his efforts. He had the walkie-talkie strapped on his hip, which had played little role so far. The head constable returned to say that the governor's helicopter had just appeared over the airport, and that the motorcade was expected on schedule.

The picket line appeared to be as steady as it was when I first arrived at the spot, and I felt the time had come for us to do something instead of just waiting. Otherwise we might not have enough time to deal with any problem that arose after we started our action to clear the picketers. I took another look around and started purposefully towards where the ACP stood, admiring his reflection in the rear-view mirror of his jeep. I was intercepted by the elderly head constable, who placed a hand on my arm, glanced at his watch and at the sky, and said: 'Give it another few minutes, sir.' I stopped and looked quizzically at the head constable, who smiled and replied: 'It starts suddenly to get cold at this time of the year, sir. The temperature drops in minutes as a chilly wind blows in from the hills. This happens around this time of the day in this season.'

I couldn't believe my ears. Was he seriously suggesting that we wait for a chill wind to arrive on schedule, for the temperature to drop sharply, and for the protesters to melt away? His expression indicated that that was precisely what he thought. I peered through the deepening gloom, although it was just 3:45 p.m. by my watch. I looked up anxiously as I heard what sounded like the wail of a siren, coming from the direction of the road from the airport. But it was only an ambulance hurrying to the Raj Bhavan, where it would be stationed as long as the governor was in residence. I glanced down at my watch again, for want of anything better to do, and decided that we would have to act. I then felt the head constable's hand on my arm again, and I looked in the direction he was pointing. Despite screwing up my eyes, rubbing them and staring again, I could see nothing. It was some time before I realized that I could see nothing on the road because there was no one there!

The chilly wind had arrived at exactly the time the head constable had predicted, leading the protestors to leave for their homes. I asked for a few policemen to go down the avenue and check that there was no one lurking near the gates. The head constable barked an order and ten men detached themselves from the second line and went in double-march time down the road. After a few minutes, the men came back to report that the road was clear. With a sigh of relief, I walked to the centre of the broad avenue and standing in the middle, arms akimbo, surveyed the scene. Street lights started to come on, as had the bright flood lights of the Raj Bhavan compound, which was a high-security zone. The sodium vapour lamps cast their golden pools of light over the darkened road, the moat to one side, and the high walls on the other.

The distant wail of sirens indicated that the motorcade was approaching. Soon, several sirens could be distinguished from one another. I looked down the road, and the beams of the lead vehicle cut a bright swathe in the darkness, followed by more beams, and soon, the rapidly moving convoy was gliding smartly down the avenue. The gates were flung open, the policemen stood stiffly to attention, the vehicles turned into the drive, and even the ACP finally appeared to condescend to acknowledge the situation around him by standing in a pose that approximated to being 'at attention'.

And that was how the episode of the Raj Bhavan picket line came to a satisfactory conclusion, thanks to a chilly wind that arrived on time.

Imphal Evenings

As the day wound down, figures moved about on the veranda rather more slowly than earlier in the day. Sitting across me, the superintendent fidgeted as he furtively glanced at his wristwatch once again to confirm that his customary closing time had arrived while I seemed oblivious to that fact. To a mind accustomed to the importance of certain marker events in a typical working day – signing the attendance register on arrival, the morning cup of tea followed by meticulously prepared paan, the lunch eaten out of the tiffin box carefully packed by his wife, the post-lunch siesta, the afternoon cup of refreshing tea followed by another paan, and most importantly, the closing up for the day – this casual approach to the important steps marking the end of a working day was not easy to accept.

This last matter was the most weighty one of all, a task that required care and diligence, and hence much more time than I, for one, felt necessary. It commenced about an hour before the office closed, during which time all work would be suspended, and those waiting to enquire about various matters would be informed that they would have to return the next day. An interminable process involving sounds of scraping, squawking and squealing of the office furniture would follow with cupboards, desks, drawers and doors being moved around, opened, closed, unlocked and relocked. Finally, all would be silent as the last scooter sputtered out of the DC's office compound to join the rest of the traffic in the narrow streets of Imphal.

Once I had finally relieved the superintendent of his misery, I sat back, enjoying the silence, allowing it to flow over me. It was quite dark outside, and the lights were already switched on. I did not feel like writing the final orders in several cases that I had finished hearing. I called the ADM on the intercom, and finding him still at his office, strolled across, passing through long deserted corridors strewn with scraps of paper, blood-red paan stains on the walls.

Entering the brightly lit room of the ADM, I smiled a greeting at the rangy figure sprawled in his usual fashion behind the large desk, managing to give the impression that he was draped on an easy chair instead of a stiff-backed one in his office. As I entered, he deposited a wad of paan in a corner of his mouth, all the while speaking into the phone, and gestured to me to take one for myself. I was not given to the habit of chewing paan, but did not mind one on occasion, and taking one from the packet, I confirmed that it did not have tobacco before placing it in my mouth.

The ADM placed the receiver back on the rest and yawned and stretched as he said, 'Arre yaar, what a day! Hearing after hearing through the day. I must have sat through at least fifteen without a single bloody adjournment request. Several times I was tempted to ask them whether they wanted an adjournment, although both parties were present with their lawyers, just to see what will happen. The problem about completing hearings is that we have to write the bloody judgments, which is a pain in the arse. I like the dictation, though,' he said, referring to his demure stenographer whose clothes fit a shade too snugly.

I smiled as I regarded the handsome grinning face of the ADM, and could very well understand the confusion of the stenographer, who must be torn between resisting and revelling in the undivided attention of the handsome man across the desk.

'What about another game of Scrabble? I feel like winning another bottle of Scotch. Are you busy?' I asked. The ADM delightedly agreed and bustled about, getting his things together to leave. We agreed to meet at his place in thirty minutes and I returned to my office, collected my attaché case and climbed into the old jeep Rajen had brought round to the porch.

A short while later, I was at the ADM's house, a C-type quarters with a little garden. Parking my jeep outside the gate, I walked up the drive, past carefully tended beds of flowering plants, and climbed the steps to the little veranda where orchids hung from pots suspended on wires. The ADM's vivacious wife who was away in Delhi prided herself on her house and garden. I stepped into the well-furnished and comfortable drawing room and allowed the warmth to seep through to my limbs. Sinking into the large sofa, I waited for the ADM. The Scrabble board was already laid on the cards table, four chairs arranged around it, with the little racks for placing the pieces in front of each player, the notepad and pencil for keeping the tally, and the coasters for glasses that would hold the drinks. On a side table were a half-full bottle of Johnnie Walker Red Label, another of Old Monk rum, a couple of bottles of soda and a bucket of ice. The fat Chambers dictionary that would definitely come into play several times during the long encounter ahead reposed alongside. We were all set to do battle on the field of words.

The ADM entered rubbing his hands, looking smart in a fresh T-shirt and corduroys, with chappals. He radiated health, wealth and a certain sangfroid that stopped well short of smugness. He enjoyed being comfortable, was unapologetic about it, and took every opportunity to share what he had with friends. His guileless, smiling face disarmed most people, and I genuinely liked him. If caught out on something he had said that was not true, he would laugh and accept the correction without any difficulty. He was quite unapologetic about using his vast network of friends to get a good posting, and this somehow made it all right since there was nothing covert about what he did. He was always willing to share information that was of use to another, quite unlike the typical bureaucrat.

After slipping a cassette of Mehdi Hassan into the tape recorder, he poured two large pegs of rum into the glasses, added the soda and ice, and brought it over to where I was sitting engrossed in an old issue of *Playboy*. The rum felt nice and warm as it went down my throat, and my mood lightened almost immediately. The other had taken his seat at the table with the Scrabble set, and was engaged in the preliminary preparations and checking that everything we needed was there. Just then, another vehicle drew up outside, and several pairs of feet could be heard on the steps. The door was flung open and greetings rent the air as two more men followed a couple of ladies into the room. I stood up to greet them, smiled when I saw who they were, and decided that it was going to be an interesting evening. The banter between the company present was mostly in Hindi, a language I managed as well, lapsing into English when I failed to get the right word.

I recall the time my parents visited me in Imphal, just a couple of months earlier, and we were invited to the house of a senior officer for dinner. The hostess conducted an animated conversation with my mother entirely in Hindi, although she spoke excellent English, having been educated at one of the best girls' schools in north India. My mother listened to her patiently with a smile, and said at the end that she hadn't understood a word the other had spoken. The news being conveyed with a smile, everybody was stunned into laughter. The ladies continued the conversation in English for the rest of the evening!

The four of us who enjoyed Scrabble sat round the table, and the game was soon proceeding in earnest, with the usual disputes and challenges. The two ladies who were not playing sat and talked a little apart from us, about recent visits from the mainland, an impending vacation or official trip to Delhi, a detailed description of newcomers who had recently moved into the locality, and the usual trivia characteristic of life in a residential enclave far from home. The ADM rose once more to refill the glasses, and returned with a stricken expression to inform the shocked gathering that the liquor had run out – an unmitigated disaster!

There was nothing to be done but to go out and get another bottle. The likely sources were all ruled out for one reason or the other, and the faces of all grew longer and more strained. Unable to stand it any longer, I got to my feet and, pulling on my jacket, headed for the door. The ADM divined my intentions. He too grabbed his jacket and cap and hastened after me. We climbed into my jeep and roared off into the night. I was not sure where we were headed, but vaguely understood that a bootlegger located in Singjamei was the only one likely to be open at that ungodly hour.

The wind stung the exposed parts of our being as we drove down deserted streets. The headlamps picked out masses of insects with their glittering bodies as they launched into suicidal dives in the brilliant beams. We passed a couple of police pickets, which appeared to be deserted since we were not challenged. Soon, we were at our destination. The shop seemed to be closed, and I wondered whether our mission was in vain. However, the ADM pointed towards the bottom of the shop shutters, and I could discern a sliver of light escaping through the narrow gap, indicating that there was someone in the shop. He remained in the jeep, hugging himself to ward off the biting cold, while I banged on the wooden shutters. A guttural voice enquired in Manipuri what the hell I wanted. On hearing my requirement spoken in Hindi, a section of the shutter parted to reveal a brilliant shaft of light. A bleary pair of eyes regarded me for a long moment, a beedi drooping out of a corner of the clamped jaws. The face then disappeared, only to reappear after a couple of minutes. The price was barked out and once the payment was placed in the slot, taken inside and counted, a bottle slowly appeared through the same opening. I picked it up and returned to the jeep, a halo (made brighter by the milky street light) surrounding it thanks to the ADM's luxuriant cigarette smoke.

As we accelerated down the road, a thought appeared to strike the ADM. He became still and looked around at the deserted streets. He spoke, 'Do you know why the place is so bloody quiet and desolate?' I merely grunted, being too intent on trying to see the road ahead through the dirty windscreen. He continued, 'That's because we're in Singjamei, dammit. The fucking nerve centre of the insurgents. Even during daytime, only well-armed soldiers in platoon strength patrol this locality.'

And there we were, two slightly tipsy district officials, in a vehicle with official markings, weaponless, on a mission to procure a bottle of rum! We began to laugh uproariously, and slightly hysterically, as we left Singjamei and came to a less dangerous and better-lit area. Humming at first, and then recalling the words, we started to sing the IAS song: '*Aao karmathey veer, aao dharmathey dheer, aao unnathey sheer, naahi bhoyy ...*' Exotic insects of the night continued to mindlessly hurl themselves to their deaths against the bright headlamps of the jeep as we headed home, our voices raised in song.

Nair-saab and His Marvellous Jeep

Where on earth are we? I thought as we walked through quiet rooms filled with gleaming equipment. It appeared as if we were in a sci-fi movie set. Smooth linoleum-covered floors in a pastel shade of greyish blue set off the off-white walls lined from floor to ceiling with absorbent tiles with their distinctive pockmarks. Bright fluorescent lamps were arrayed in neat rows on the ceiling, illuminating the rooms with shadowless lighting. We padded silently through the rooms, our feet shod in rubber slippers provided at the entrance. Prominent signs in stencilled lettering informed us about the activity going on in each room we passed, and also at each workstation. Some of the information was in the usual military acronyms that made little sense to the uninitiated.

We were in the Police Wireless Centre as part of our introduction to the way the police in Manipur conducted their work. We were not overly excited when we set off that morning from the Circuit House, expecting to be treated to a dreary and droning lecture by a bored officer. We drove into a compound deep inside the headquarters of the 1st Battalion of Manipur Rifles and found ourselves alighting on a gravelled drive with well-cared-for lawns and flower beds lining it. Entering a low-slung building with corrugated-sheet roofing, we found ourselves in a lobby where an officer received us, briefed us about the day's programme and led us into the air-conditioned coolness of a large space. The far side was occupied by cubicles – each of which had a desk with wireless transmission equipment – set against the wall. Most were occupied by men and women who murmured softly into mikes set on short stands while little lights played on the consoles on the wall. Notes were scribbled on pads, and pages torn off and placed in trays. These were periodically emptied by a man who would gather up the transcribed messages and take them to the officer on duty. It all looked very professional and businesslike. And in complete contrast to what we had seen ever since we arrived in Imphal.

So what was this all about? Were we in some hush-hush military or intelligence establishment that was engaged in listening in on radio transmissions from across the border? The set-up definitely did not reflect what we had seen of the administration in this place, which displayed the trademark sloppiness and slipshod manner of government establishments everywhere in India: dusty rooms and furniture, worn-out carpets, frayed and sagging curtains, windows with panes missing, the omnipresent betel nut stains.

More striking was the manner of the people working there. Their polite and purposeful look as they went about the task of briefing us about the work that went on in the facility stood out in marked contrast to the shambling and obviously unrehearsed briefings we had been subjected to on previous occasions. These chaps not only seemed to know what they were about but appeared to have prepared for the training, and seemed to take pride in explaining the work they did. All quite baffling to us as we found ourselves, against our will, getting interested in the work they did.

The facility was the nerve centre of the wireless communications network of the police in Manipur – hundreds of wireless messages went out or were received every hour of the day to and from police outposts in remote parts of the state, many inaccessible by road and more than a day's march from the nearest road. A stream of messages came in that had to be sorted and sent at regular intervals to various parts of the police establishment in Imphal. This was accomplished by a team of motorcycle dispatch riders who would roar off in a muffled drumbeat of sound after being handed over a bag of messages. The sound of a Royal Enfield Bullet revving its engine never failed to send a thrill through me, reminding me of a childhood in the tea and rubber plantations, where managers went about the hill tracks on these powerful machines.

As we went from room to room, it was clear that thought and intelligence were at work, planning, monitoring, and controlling what went on. When we were ultimately ushered into a neat and well-appointed office, we met the man responsible for this achievement – N.K. Nair, superintendent of police (SP) (wireless), as the sign on the desk informed us. Nair was a strapping, square-jawed man, dressed in a well-pressed uniform, fortyish, with flecks of grey in his hair that was closely cropped in the regulation military style. A trimmed moustache – universally sported by the Malayali male – adorned his upper lip, framing a mouth that had a ready smile. Nair-saab, as we were to discover in the weeks and months that followed that first meeting, smiled and laughed a lot, which was another strange thing about the man, in a place where very few of the mayangs appeared to have much to smile about. His uninhibited laughter would be startling to one who heard it the first time, but you soon came to expect it, not only as a response to something funny, but also as a means of punctuating something which was not in the least bit funny.

We arranged ourselves around a large table, to one side of which was placed a large map of Manipur. Using a pointer, Nair-saab explained in a clear, parade-ground voice the features of the wireless communications network in Manipur. As the narrative progressed, it became apparent that considerable ingenuity had gone into fashioning what was acknowledged to be one of the finest police communications networks in the country. We were taken methodically through the difficulties involved in establishing a communications network using wireless transmitters in a terrain as inhospitable as that of Manipur. Such devices apparently worked on the line-of-sight principle, and so it was necessary to place repeater stations at vantage points on mountain peaks to ensure that signals were carried to all parts of the state. What Nair-saab did was to go one step further and provide a system that enabled a transmitter in any part of the state to speak to another in any other part. This was accomplished through a cunningly designed system of passive repeater sets, placed atop trees in vantage points. These had batteries that needed to be changed periodically, but beyond that, the devices needed little maintenance. They were not easy to disrupt and intercept because their location was known only to Nair-saab and his team.

As he told me one evening, the National Police Commission headed by Dharma Vira had applauded his efforts and held up his accomplishment as a fine example of what could be achieved with intelligence, skill and commitment even on a shoestring budget. When Nair recounted this, there was no trace of boasting but just a quiet pride and satisfaction at a job well done. Everything he did reflected this pride, and it was a pleasure being shown round his little garden which was his pride and joy. The small fish pond in the corner had been converted into a pocket pisciculture project, and one had to endure a long but interesting lecture on the difficulties of rearing different varieties of fish in the clayey soil of Imphal, with its peculiar mineral endowment and properties.

After the visit, and my attachment to the police as part of my probation, I kept in touch with Nair-saab and his family. His wife, two daughters and little son completed the family that he was so fond of. His home reflected the same passion for detail that was evident at the wireless centre. Regulation PWD-supply furniture had been cleverly arranged and covered with local fabric to create a cosy home that I enjoyed visiting – which I did at least a couple of times every week as long as I was in Imphal. While the main attraction was the delicious Malayali food that Mrs Nair prepared (especially the fish!), I enjoyed the conversation which was always interesting, given Nair-saab's enthusiasm for technology and thirst for knowledge. As we discussed or argued about some aspect of technology, Mrs Nair would potter about, caring for the family, or sit quietly knitting in a corner, occasionally joining in the conversation if something interested her. There was a warmth and calm about her that contributed to building the home that the otherwise featureless quarters had become. Every time I stepped out into the chilly night to walk the short distance through the senior officers' colony in Sanjenthong across the bridge back to the Circuit House, a wistfulness would come over me as I turned to look at the Nairs framed in the bright light of the open doorway as they waved goodbye. How special and inviting was a home even to a visitor, I thought, and how uninviting was even the most well-appointed house if it was not a home?

One evening, a couple of junior officers and I were at the residence of the CS, sipping fine whisky, when the telephone trilled. It appeared from the brief exchange that a fire had broken out at the border crossing at Moreh and there were some casualties and damage to property. The CS called another number and barked into the phone: 'Please ask Nair to bring his jeep around.' We were puzzled at this strange request. The vehicle arrived in a few minutes, and we peered through the windows into the evening gloom to see the CS walk briskly down the drive and get into the jeep. He sat in it for about fifteen minutes and then rejoined us. Unable to restrain our curiosity and emboldened by the whisky I asked, 'Sir, what were you doing in the jeep?' The CS took a sip from his glass and grinned. 'Oh, you noticed the jeep. That, my dear fellow, is the wonder vehicle, the "chitty chitty bang bang" of Manipur. That jeep is rigged so one can speak to any place in Manipur, with total clarity and privacy. I guess you fellows have been to Nair's police wireless set-up. He's a marvel, that Nair. I don't know what I or indeed the entire administration here would do without him. I was able to speak to the BSF commandant at Moreh and get a full report on what happened and what's being done.'

We looked out of the window at the jeep that had reversed

and was now vanishing from sight. Our thoughts went back to the gleaming facility that housed the centre of the wireless web that bound this mountainous territory together, with its invisible filaments finer and stronger than any spider's gossamer masterpiece, crossing mountains and deep valleys, connecting wireless sets hidden high on treetops, leaping from one set to the other across dense forests and raging torrents, carrying the daily traffic of messages that make up the stuff of modern governance. And all of it had been conjured out of meagre resources. More than the technical virtuosity behind the achievement, I suspect what we marvelled at was the positive energy that radiated from Nair-saab, utterly unaffected by being far away from his home state. He did not need an external socket to plug his power cord into to draw the energy he needed to carry on with his work and life. He carried a portable generator inside him which must have been solar- or nuclear-powered, for it never appeared to stop working, and in fact continuously radiated energy, warmth and cheer.

Nair-saab was a living testimony to the view that there is never anything wrong with the people; it is always the leadership one should fault. Most people, especially the outsiders I encountered in Manipur, clearly looked like they would rather be elsewhere, and this 'loser' quality hung like a bad smell around them. This outlook was reflected in everything they said and did, and naturally affected the quality of their work. It is a singular misfortune to work under such a person, and I could well understand the low spirits of people in such departments and offices. Time and again have I come across cases where a new officer has been able to transform a non-performing office. How was this magic accomplished? The staff was the same, so were the incentives or lack thereof, and the work processes. Of course, competence of the person heading the office is necessary, but I am sure it was not a sufficient condition. Something more was needed, something that would catalyse people trapped in a low-performance equilibrium to take their work to a higher level.

Over the years, I have read much on the subject of improving the quality of governance, and found much that had to do with the usual incentive structures such as higher pay, better working conditions and better training. I have no doubt that these will help improve matters, but I am equally certain that relying on just these and similar measures will only improve the cost of governance steeply, with little to show by way of superior outcomes.

Through my years as a junior government officer, and later as a businessman, I have come across many people like Nair-saab who were driven by something quite different, who always appeared to be eager to figure out what could be done, instead of concluding that something could not be done. Despite the extent of corruption in India, if we are still functioning as a nation and a democracy after sixty years, surely one of the reasons has to be the fact that there are many Nair-saabs working in government at various levels.

The Jain Book Store

Rajen Singh gunned the engine impatiently as he waited for me to cover the distance from my office, down the long passage, through the large waiting area, and finally out into the porch of the DC's office. I hated this habit of his, as the old jeep belched oily smoke from its innards suggesting it had too many major afflictions for anything useful to be done to prolong its life in the local workshop. But like many things Rajen did, this cursed habit was hard to exorcise, much like the odd affectation of cyclists who reverse their pedals rapidly while coasting along slowly or going downhill. It serves no apparent purpose, but seems to satisfy some inner craving.

Rajen was a creature of habit. In the morning, when he arrived to drive me to work, he would select the direction to take after leaving the house based purely on arbitrary selection. Any other time during the day, he would sit gunning the engine and ask where I wanted to go. In the evening, he would ask, 'Home or Jain Book Store, sir?' That day, I selected the latter, and the jeep went down the roughly surfaced road, scattering the hens and children playing there.

Shoppers would throng Paona Bazaar at that time of the day, trying to get the shopping done before it got too chilly or late. The last rickshaws would pick up passengers not later than 7 p.m., and if one missed those, it meant a long trudge home, carrying the day's shopping. The jeep halted opposite a little bookshop bearing the prominent sign: P. JAIN BOOK STORE. It boasted one shutter, but ran deep into the back of the three-storeyed building. On either side were a hardware shop and a hairdresser. The former would begin to shut shop rather early as it was no small task to store all the cans of paint, faucets, bath fittings and other goods that the enterprising shopkeeper displayed, having commandeered a portion of the sidewalk for his use. The hairdresser's establishment was a brightly lit affair, with three swivel chairs arrayed in front of large mirrors running along the length of the wall above a shiny laminated counter that was neatly arranged with the tools of his trade. Little bulbs around the name board flickered on and off according to a rhythm which no one had figured out to date. Loud music filtered out of the half-swing doors, and when there were no customers, the cheery owner and staff could be seen through the glass windows, exchanging banter over the assorted film magazines or chatting with passers-by.

The Jain Book Store was a more staid establishment which mostly dealt in textbooks for schools and colleges. These occupied most of the display shelf space. Towards the rear were a few shelves of other books for the genuine book lover. The owner, Mr Jain, did not grudge this kind of customer browsing time, and when business was not brisk, would saunter over to exchange views about the books with anyone browsing there at the time. Although the display was not extensive, Mr Jain would order books for his regular buyers; and he always managed to get this done in a remarkably short time, considering the transportation problems at Imphal and the condition of the overworked postal department at the time. Mr Jain always sported a severe expression, which he probably felt suited an owner of an academic bookshop, and so he was mostly attired in dark coat and trousers, with rimless spectacles perched at the tip of his thin long nose adding to the severity of his mien.

But, in this case at least, appearances were deceptive, as Mr Jain was the most gentle and kind-hearted person I had come across in

Imphal. I often wondered how he made ends meet in his business as he fell hook, line, and sinker for every hard-luck story spun by an enterprising schoolteacher or college librarian when asked to pay for a consignment. After sympathetically listening to a painful account of a school struggling gamely to make ends meet in order to ensure that the sacred mission of teaching the children was not affected, Mr Jain would briskly bring the discussion to an end saying, 'All right. I will give you one more month to pay. Not a day more,' leaving a delighted chap who had not dared to hope that he would get more than a week's extension!

The shop did not attract the casual buyer, and other than the regulars, the only ones who came in were those who mistook it for a regular bookshop. This happened about a couple of times every day, and it was amusing to see how Mr Jain would patiently explain that his was an academic bookshop.

As usual, when he saw my jeep, Mr Jain would come over to the street to welcome me in. Although onlookers would attribute that deference to the large sign on the bumper of the vehicle which proclaimed 'SDO, IMPHAL WEST', it was more due to the fact that Mr Jain put me in the select category of those who truly appreciated books.

On one such visit, his brow furrowed as he escorted me into the shop and led the way to the rear where the shelves that interested me stood. 'I'm afraid the Koestler you asked for has not arrived. I am not able to understand the delay. I have sent a reminder and hope it will come within a week,' he added apologetically. Brightening up as he spotted another book, he reached up. 'However, I have another book that I recall you mentioning some time back.' He held it out with a smile, and I was glad when I saw that it was *The Ochre Robe* by Leopold Fisher, aka Agehananda Bharati. I liked the hard cover it came with, and noting the price, said I would take it. The tinkling of the little bell over the entrance announced another arrival, and he went off to attend to the other customer. I idly leafed through the book, pausing to read a passage in some detail.

'His description of the meeting with the Sankaracharya of Kanchi is interesting, in the sense it gives you a flavour of the kind of man Fisher was, as well as a peep into the mind of one of the remarkable minds of our time.' This was spoken in a quiet voice, with excellent English diction. I turned to look at the speaker and saw a trim, youngish chap about the same age as me, with a studious, almost scholarly, expression on his bespectacled, clean-shaven face.

'I have heard about this book, and also about Fisher, and that is the reason for taking it. However, I hope I learn something about the man and that it is not too much about Vedic Hinduism,' I responded. 'Aren't you interested in Vedic Hinduism?' enquired the stranger. 'Personally, I find it interesting, especially when it is treated in relation to the society of the time and not uprooted from its social and historical context. When that happens, it becomes just another scholarly work with dense passages of incomprehensible syllogisms and mental acrobatics that leave my head spinning,' he added with a grin.

'Have you read *Autobiography of a Yogi*?' I asked. He nodded by way of reply. 'What did you think about that book?' I continued. 'Yogananda Paramahamsa takes one through a remarkable personal journey which I for one believe we must take seriously if one is to get an inside view of his mind. If one applies rational criteria to what he describes, and views them in a phenomenological sense, then they are too fantastic to be taken seriously, figments of the writer's imagination, creations of either a demented or a hallucinating mind. And that is how I see that book. And that is why I consider him on the same plane as that other remarkable explorer of the human mind, Aurobindo, who intuitively mapped out man's inner space in a more comprehensive and fascinating way than anyone has ever attempted before or since.'

Our conversation ebbed and flowed and continued pleasantly, and it was only when Mr Jain politely coughed to draw our attention to the fact that it was almost closing time that we realized how time had flown. Turning to take leave of my new friend, I introduced myself. 'I know you. Your jeep says it all,' he replied, and stepped out into the night.

In the days and weeks that followed, my visits to Mr Jain's bookshop were enlivened by the discussions with this interesting and enigmatic young man on books, and through them, many and varied fields of human endeavour. We were very different – in our outlook, our beliefs, our backgrounds – but in a curious way, quite similar. Like him, I too valued the Marxian approach as one of the few truly scientific ways to approach the study of man in history, in society, and in economic relationships; I too abhorred injustice in any form, and never tried to defend the indefensible, regardless of the impact of such a stand on things I valued; I too, being young, was optimistic that the golden age of man lay in the future, not in some imaginary past, that it would be built by the endeavour of humanity as a whole. In short, we were young, and full of hope, despite the dispiriting things we saw every day around us, and it was only in the unimportant things that we differed.

One day, while I was collecting my copy of *The Resistance*, my bookstore friend said, 'I am curious to see that you read this magazine. Why do you read it?' I replied that I honestly felt it was the only intelligent piece of writing that I had come across on matters concerning the north-east in general, and Manipur in particular. I liked the sophistication and honesty of the analysis, and the willingness to face up to facts even when they were inconvenient. He smiled and nodded that he understood very well what I meant.

'Don't you get the impression that the stories about the north-east filed by journalists in the mainland dailies appear to be written by people who've never actually been here and seen things the way they are? As if they sat in their hotel rooms in Calcutta and wrote the story? Or, if they did actually travel to Imphal or Kohima or Aizawl, they interviewed an official in his office and headed straight back? Journalists are supposed to be curious about what lies below the surface, keen on ferreting out facts, smelling out leads and assiduously following them. Here, they seem either disinterested or afraid to go after the real story.' We stood engrossed in our discussion while the street outside rapidly emptied itself as darkness fell.

I found myself thinking about my companion's words and realized that the stories carried by the mainland dailies had a curious sameness to them, despite the differences in editorial outlook of at least a couple of them. But when it came to the stories of his region, something seemed to eliminate differences in viewpoints, imposing a uniformity that seemed to derive from looking through the same tinted lenses. I suggested that it was perhaps due to the restrictions on travel in the region imposed by the authorities, or the disturbed conditions, or the perceived hostility towards outsiders, or the difficulties in travelling from point to point, or maybe just a combination of all these that persuaded otherwise diligent journalists to be content with an interview or official press release. But I wondered why the editors of these newspapers were satisfied with these stories when it was clear that they did not reflect the ground realities.

My companion's take was interesting. 'Perhaps it is because the north-east is like a foreign country. Look at the stories filed from places like Washington, London, Moscow or Tokyo in Indian newspapers. Most are of course from news agencies. But even those that appear to be filed by correspondents … do you get the sense that those who filed them wore their shoes out tramping the backstreets of those cities trying to get the real story behind the "official" one? Don't you see a young man or woman trying to justify the expense of their assignment or stick to the commitment of filing a story every week, milking the same source every time, usually over dinner or a drink, trying to stay authentic while imparting something different to this week's dispatch? Being in a foreign country has something special to it, which makes one behave differently. This probably affects journalists too.'

I pondered over this and tried to remember my only trip abroad, to Singapore, Hong Kong and Tokyo the previous year. The sense of being an alien shocked me, despite my extensive reading about those places. The differences manifest everywhere reinforced this sense of alienness – in the appearance of the people, the language they spoke, the food they ate, the way they dressed. I realized that these factors were active in the case of a mainlander visiting the north-east, where everything he saw looked different. The visitor could very well have been in Burma or Laos for all the identification he would make with what he saw and heard and experienced.

'Is it language that primarily separates people?' I asked. 'What really makes a person feel alien somewhere?'

'Language probably contributes much. But it does not work alone. Other factors have to come into play. For instance, if you were in Orissa and don't speak a word of Oriya I'm sure you will still not feel an alien, because a person from Kerala looks much like one from Orissa, especially in the towns and cities. When there are other significant differences in the way people look or dress, language completes the sense of being different, introducing a barrier that prevents genuine intercourse. Even where you find someone who speaks your language but not as a native speaker, the lack of proper non-verbal communication makes it that much more difficult to pick up nuances and subtle but important differences in meaning and emphasis. It will be curiously like listening to a memorized speech, where you get the strong impression that these are not the speaker's words! That's probably the role language plays in exaggerating differences. And that could be one reason why dividing India on linguistic lines after 1956 seems to have been a logical step.'

I was struck by something he said and replied: 'Language appears to be more important than we imagine. It enables us to go behind the façade and touch the person we are speaking with. Communication is established once the language barrier

is breached through any means. But, when language is merely
one of a set of several barriers such as colour, appearance, dress,
custom, food, even climate, the feeling of alienness is complete.
I recall going to a village in western UP as part of the training
at Mussoorie, and the sense of being an alien that I felt in the
house of a Jat farmer as I sat on a stool with all these tall, swarthy,
tanned men lounging around in their kurta–pyjamas, speaking in
a dialect I could not understand. It was the first time I personally
experienced the bonds of nationhood being tested.'

He smiled. 'That's exactly what I mean. If you were a journalist
travelling in that part of UP and heard about an atrocity against a
Harijan family in that village, would you be willing to or be able
to ferret around in that village to discover what really happened?
There is an opacity to life in such places, and a peep behind this
opaque veil is not vouchsafed to you or me who are not of that
place and community, and so we will never really be able to
apprehend the reality of what goes on there. Can you imagine an
American reporter succeeding in getting to the truth of an inter-
caste dispute in an interior village in Tamil Nadu, especially if he
does not speak Tamil?'

How does one work with and among people when one cannot
touch them, cannot know what they feel, cannot sense their
emotions? Is it not easier to be a representative of a 'ruling' power,
as the young British officers were in British India, where both the
ruler and the ruled know and accept the terms of the relationship?
Every action by both protagonists makes sense in this context. But
in my case, there appeared to be a difference. I thought myself to
be one of them, a fellow citizen and a member of the civil services
– a 'public servant'. They saw me as the local representative of a
colonial power, backed by all the authority and awesome power
that goes with such a description.

We spent occasional evenings at the bookshop arguing about
an article in the previous issue of the journal, and these sessions
helped fill the huge gaps in my knowledge about the region. The

contents of the journal could be held to be seditious and the author would obviously be liable to be prosecuted for violating several laws, not least among them being the active promotion of the interests of the underground movement.

It was only later that I saw what he meant and realized that, in the north-east, what really keeps us apart is the illusion of shared nationhood. The embrace of 'Mother India' was probably too overwhelming. A measure of autonomy given to the local governments would probably have yielded a better harvest in terms of peace, economic development and a better life for the people.

Cultural Exchange

As I climbed into the jeep, Rajen Singh swung the vehicle smartly around in a racing turn with a squeal of worn tyres on the rough road and drove off with a grinding of gears. I sighed at the noises of protest made by the vehicle, which always set my teeth on edge. After a few unsuccessful attempts to change Rajen's approach to driving to something that was more in line with my father's (and since I had trained under his watchful eyes, mine) style, I had reconciled myself to allowing the latter to indulge his Formula One technique, deciding instead to rely on the power of prayer and sorcery to ward off the threat to life and limb.

The second reason for my philosophical sigh was that Rajen accelerated away in the direction he arbitrarily chose without enquiring about the programme for the day. If one turned left on leaving the compound, one was heading away from town; turning right meant going to the town and my office in the deputy commissioner's office complex. By the time I pointed out that we were headed the wrong way, a fair distance would have been covered. Without batting an eyelid, Rajen would swing the vehicle around in the middle of the road in a U-turn that would have raised an appreciative roar from spectators at Le Mans.

That day, the schedule included an inspection of the SDC's office at Thoubal, followed by an inspection at a disputed pathway. The drive would be over open country, along the flat open plain of the Central District. It was a relief to get out of the densely packed town and I watched the rice paddies flash by in shades of emerald and opal, with occasional flashes of silver as water-flooded fields reflected the sun's brilliance.

Rajen Singh, in addition to being a closet F-1 driver, was also an incurable prattler. It was therefore not long before he started to recount the happenings since we parted the previous evening. I never ceased to marvel at the number of things that seemed to happen below the placid surface of town life in Imphal. Things were quiet on the elopement front now that summer was over. Autumn was well advanced and there were hints of winter in the cold air that rushed down the mountains in the evenings.

Rajen Singh's choice of subject for the day was the impending wedding of the daughter of Agarwal the rice merchant with the son of a Marwari trader from Guwahati. Rajen was apparently privy to the financial minutiae of both families and proceeded to inform me about the Croesus's palace-like splendour of the groom's father's dwelling. After a detailed description that neglected no room of the said dwelling, he moved on to an inventory of the fixed and movable assets of the family. I wondered whether the income tax department would have even a fraction of the information that was being served in such intimate detail by Rajen Singh.

After exhausting the narrative potential of the apparently limitless wealth of the groom's family, he turned to the local rice merchant, who I was certain must be suffering from severe feelings of inadequacy in the face of such immense affluence. But I was informed with much relish by Rajen about the fabulous riches of Mr Agarwal. This admittedly came as a surprise to me, since I had had occasion to see for myself the shops and residence of the latter on a few occasions when searching for secret hoards of rice under the Essential Commodities Act. I did not bother to argue with Rajen Singh who was by now firing on all cylinders, both in his narrative as well as behind the wheel of the jeep.

Rajen paused in his narrative while he slowed to a crawl to thread his way through a herd of cattle. Manipuri drivers had this almost superstitious dread of hurting animals, especially cows, while driving, unlike their counterparts in other parts of India who merely pressed the horn while roaring through the herd. The complicated exercise having been completed to his satisfaction, the brief interlude of quiet came to an end with the roar of the jeep matching the shouted voice of Rajen Singh. Although I was somewhat familiar with north Indian wedding rituals, I had to suffer through a blow-by-blow account of the wedding ceremony, as understood by the narrator.

We were now entering a village, and Rajen Singh acknowledged that fact by keeping his right hand glued to the horn as we flashed through narrow lanes. I shut my eyes tightly, praying that we did not hit anything – human, animal or inanimate. We drew to a halt with a dramatic screeching, and through the cloud of dust thrown up by our grand arrival, could discern the figures of the SDC and his staff waiting to receive us. I climbed out stiffly, and after finding that I was still able to move my limbs, walked stiff-legged towards the waiting group.

A short, dapper and severe-looking man, the SDC stepped forward and welcomed me with a flowery speech delivered without expression. After standing in embarrassed silence, trying not to meet the speaker's eye, my gaze went from face to face in the motley group solemnly looking back at me. I gathered that they did not understand a word of what the SDC was saying, since he spoke in English! When he finally came to the end of his speech, the group broke into loyal applause, more at his effort of reciting a long speech from memory than from any happiness at seeing me. By now, having understood the customs of the place, I thanked the SDC for the warm welcome and in a few well-chosen words, hoped that the inspection would reveal a well-run office. At this, the SDC looked tense, while the rest of the welcome party, figuring that the pause called for applause, broke into a volley of warm handclaps and broad smiles. The SDC gave them a withering look, his expression indicating that they would not be smiling if they understood what I had said.

I was ushered into a neat little building of the usual 'Assam-type' construction. The walls were whitewashed and clean, and the compound free of the usual shrubs and bushes that grew so prolifically in the fertile soil and where the water table was just below the surface. It must have taken quite a bit of effort to keep the area plant-free, and I felt I could expect a tightly run office. I entered the SDC's room and my first impression was not disappointing. The room was neat, if a bit on the severe side, bare but tidy, with everything in its place. The desk, covered in the usual green cloth, was adorned with just the two 'IN' and 'OUT' trays, and a polished bell that could be punched to produce a tinkling sound to summon the lambu. On the wall were the official Government of Manipur calendar, a map of India and a photograph of Tagore. I was puzzled at the photograph, since it was de rigueur for government offices to have a picture of Gandhi or of the first president or prime minister of India. It was then that it struck me that the SDC was a proud Bengali, asserting his identity even in a remote outpost.

A cup of steaming tea was placed in front of me, as were ingenious leaf bowls – made from stitched leaves with such expertise as to even be able to hold liquids – containing pakoras and 'mixture'. I decided to stick to the safety of the 'mixture', taking a sprinkling between the fingers of one hand. The tea was drunk in silence. Then the SDC briskly set before me the various registers that would have to be inspected. A glance at the first of these registers indicated that I would find everything in order and up to date, and as that cheered me up somewhat, I made a mental note to commend the SDC on running a good office.

Inspections have their own dynamics, with subtle feedback mechanisms coming into play. If one is inspecting an office where everything is in disarray, then certain faculties are switched on that detect every little error or omission or overwriting – that most suspicious of signs that indicates to the trained administrator the presence of a more serious problem. If one knows that the office being inspected is well run, the rest of the inspection proceeds almost on autopilot, with one's mind searching for something to comment on or suggest.

It was therefore not long before I was done with the registers and files, and completed a quick walk around what turned out to be an excellent office. I complimented the SDC on several good things I noticed, about the way the record room was arranged with files in orderly rows on the slotted-angle shelves, with little cards tied to each shelf, listing out the files placed there. There is something about neatness and orderliness that appeals to all but the most insensitive mind, and I did not have to make an effort to praise what I saw as the result of systematic and regular work. The SDC's severe features appeared to soften a bit at this probably unexpected appreciation, and he began to become quite voluble, explaining little details that I might have missed. He did not forget to show me the toilet and the little kitchen, where too I remembered to commend the neatness and cleanliness.

The staff beamed at my words, nodding as I spoke, although I knew the men and women did not understand anything I said. I noticed that the SDC did not utter even a single appreciative word about the members of his staff during the entire inspection, his expression whenever one of them spoke betraying what he thought of their abilities. The finicky way he wiped his chair and table before sitting, or gingerly inspected the cup before drinking from it – as if he expected a worm to be swimming inside – reflected a desire to distance himself as much as possible from his colleagues.

The man obviously assumed that Bengalis were somehow culturally superior and this was very much in evidence in everything he did or said, for example when he sneeringly referred to the use of the Bengali script in the Manipuri language, and indeed in Assamese as well. Everything about the Manipuris displeased the SDC, from the attempts of the local people to speak Bengali, to their use of 'Indian' surnames like Singh and Sharma, to the way they wore their dhotis and kurtas or tied their turbans, or applied ash and sandalwood paste on their foreheads to denote their caste identity. To him, all these looked like efforts to mimic a superior culture.

Lunch was announced and the SDC led me back to his room, where the table had been cleared and two washed banana leaves placed along with clean steel tumblers of water. I was glad to see this, as I was quite hungry. Of course, only two places had been laid for lunch, with there being little question of the SDC deigning to eat with the others in his staff.

A lambu served a generous portion of the sticky rice grown in Manipur and added a small portion of fried fish and a chutney before ladling out chicken curry over the mound of rice. We then proceeded to eat our lunch under the attentive gaze of the rest of the office staff, who stood respectfully in a circle around us! It was not easy to eat with such an attentive audience, but I managed to finish the heaped plate with some effort. No sooner had I done so than it was refilled promptly by the alert lambu despite my protests, the rice cascading on to my hands that hovered over the banana leaf in a vain attempt to prevent the refill. There was nothing to be done but to try and eat some more, which I managed to. Seeing that there was almost half the helping still on the leaf, I wrestled with my middle-class instincts that recoiled from waste of any kind. The SDC put me out of my misery by urging me in a dry voice to leave the remaining food on the leaf if I was done, as that would indicate that I was finished. If I cleaned out the plate or leaf, it would be interpreted as a signal for a repeat helping!

With the business of lunch over, it remained only to thank the SDC for his hospitality, smile at the rest of the staff who assembled at the gate to see me off, and sit back with a contented sigh as Rajen Singh let in the clutch and we roared off in a cloud of dust.

Rajen too was silent for a brief period, no doubt digesting the lunch that he had been served in an adjoining room of the office. With furrowed brows, he appeared to be thinking. He then turned to me and asked. 'Sir, in India, are wedding ceremonies the same in the north and the south?'

I turned and looked closely at Rajen, but saw only the usual guileless expression and pleasant features. So it was not a provocative question but an entirely honest one, aimed at eliciting information that he wanted in order to fill a gap in his knowledge. I pondered about the import of the question: In India? As the jeep sped on through the flat country and people – with their distinctive eastern features – passed us as they went about their lives, suddenly, India seemed very far away. The alienness of my situation and surroundings, and the consciousness of being from a distant state came over me more forcefully than ever. A sudden gust of cold air made me pull my coat tighter around myself. As Rajen prattled on by my side, I felt more alone than I had felt in a long time.

Epilogue

W here do we go from here? What does the road ahead look like? Very different from the way it did when I first went to Imphal in 1978 – the year after the first non-Congress government was elected to office, the year of the great Andhra cyclone.

Many terrible mistakes of omission and commission have been made, with far-reaching consequences. Hundreds and possibly thousands of innocent people have paid a terrible price on account of these mistakes. While I have not been back to Imphal and the north-eastern states on account of my business preoccupations after leaving the IAS in 1983, I have been following events in those parts through the media as well as from the accounts of colleagues still working there.

As I was writing the book, I realized that I was also trying to understand what had happened all those years ago. What started out as a straightforward narrative soon became an effort at understanding the reasons for the swift decline of what was a peaceful and prosperous society into one described by a commentator as a state 'ruled from the streets by hardened street fighters'. Having been away from Manipur for nearly thirty years, and having had only sporadic contact with ex-colleagues working there, it was with shock and sadness that I read about the situation there once I left the services. The destruction of the public library and its priceless book collection by arson, 100 'bandhs' in a single year (2000), lawlessness on the streets, all point to a total collapse of governance. A more serious problem is that 'Manipur civil society is today no longer a discursive site where ideas are thrashed out and in the process consensual voices given shape and take wings (sic), but one deeply riven by numerous vested interests, each pushing its individual agendas.'[1] I found myself pondering about the larger issues that had probably escaped me in those days, and that have since come to define the trajectory of the contemporary history of the troubled north-eastern region of India.

One proposition implicit in the stories I have recounted (though I have to admit that they were chosen only for their entertainment value) is that the course of events in the north-east could have turned out very differently if many little things had been done differently. I have not been able to discern any coherent set of ideas that could approximate to a north-east policy in those days. The north-east was a 'problem' region that North Block was compelled to pay attention to, owing to its strategic location. It is my view that if small corrections had been done in the way the civil administration worked, very different outcomes could have been expected. The real issues in a local dispute would be very different from what appears to be the proximate cause when viewed from a great distance of time from the actual event. This is either due to the chronicler's conclusions creeping into the narrative, or the reader putting two and two together on the basis of contemporary realities and arriving at a quite different set of findings.

The other important proposition is that, in the late 1970s and possibly for a few years after that, government was still very much 'in charge' of the daily task of governance, not yet having abdicated that to powerful interest groups. I do not recall daily life being affected by frequent 'bandhs' and strikes. In fact, the government was quite firm in handling law and order matters, which were done

---

[1] Pradip Phanjoubam, 'In Manipur Tail Wags the Dog', *Dialogue*, April–June 2006.

by the book, sometimes comically so. If a small crowd gathered in front of the secretariat to protest, a magistrate would stand to one side politely giving the assembled crowd an opportunity to express its feelings. After a few minutes of slogan shouting, the magistrate would step forward and instruct the protesters to disperse. Upon their refusal, the magistrate would declare the assembly an unlawful one and instruct the police to remove them from the public place, whereupon the police would arrest the protesters, bundle them into a truck, and drop them off several miles out of the city to find their way back to their homes on foot! Even without the massive deployment of the military that happened in the early 1980s, the administration had a grip on governance that was evident, despite the simmering discontent and active insurgency. There was little of the siege mentality that appears to prevail these days, going by the accounts in the national media.

In many situations, if a less manipulative approach had been adopted and if there was more understanding of and sensitivity to the local tribal differences, and more finesse in the way things were handled, matters could have had quite different outcomes. Many of the episodes I recount point to the differences between the way events were perceived by the local officials and the state government, with the former rarely given a free hand to act and sort things out. Distant authority can impose its will on a remote place or event only on the basis of premeditated action. This obviously restricts the room for flexibility. If it is based on a flawed or imperfect understanding of the ground realities, it could lead to serious mistakes like those that have bedevilled the north-east. It can never match the capacity of the local administration to take into account all the facts on the ground before acting, even if only to prevent a situation from getting out of hand. One of my intentions is to bring out this disconnect between the local administration and the state capital or North Block in distant Delhi, which I believe is one of the serious flaws in the administrative machinery even today.

So what is the alternative? Is it for the state administration to leave matters more for the district administration to handle? I am fairly certain, judging from the quality of officers I encountered at various levels in the districts where I worked, that this would on the whole have definitely improved the quality of responses to a variety of local problems. What this also points to is a definite (and probably systematic) devaluing of the district administration by state governments over the past half-century, with deadly consequences on the ability of the state to understand and evolve a calibrated response to issues that could have (and indeed have had) serious long-term consequences on governance, polity and society.

What I mean is that instead of the Centre opting for a hands-off policy or a policy of exclusion of certain problem regions as a knee-jerk reaction to the situations, let it formulate a coherent policy based on equity and fairness, with one set of laws for all, applied impartially. The policy must give central place to maintaining and indeed enriching the diversity and plurality of the amazing mosaic that is India. Above all else, those in positions of power must have a commitment to the rule of law, and submit everything to the test of whether it is permitted by the law, but allow some space for flexibility after taking the ground realities into account as well. If the administration saw that their task was to implement the laws fairly and impartially, and that it was for other organs of the state to adjudicate between conflicting interests, there would not only be clarity in the roles of each such organ of the state, but an overall improvement in efficiency. I have found it effective to say: 'Look, my job is to ensure the laws are followed. If you are not happy with either my interpretation or reading of the law, you are at liberty to approach the courts for redress. I am not going to look into the relative merits of competing claims.'

I have learnt from my brief stint in the north-east the sobering lesson that the maxim 'power corrupts' is true, and has few exceptions. In his classic, *Lord of the Flies*, William Golding laid bare the savage that lurks just below the surface in all of us. I have seen how power without checks can turn the most ordinary people into monsters. A person who is secure in the knowledge that his actions will be protected from public scrutiny by the 'national security' tag will astonish even those who think they know him well by displaying casual and gratuitous cruelty.

Returning to the issue of diversity, the differences could and would have been preserved without weakening the integrity of the country or the region. The cynical manipulation of minority insecurity by exploiting a porous border to allow large numbers of people from Bangladesh to enter and gain domicile status in a region where they were previously itinerant labour whose services were in demand during the harvest season altered the demographic and political landscape irrevocably. The social consequences of this were forecast by young field officers who were my contemporaries in the north-east, but their reports remained unread and gathered dust in the state capitals or North Block; Delhi fiddled while the north-east burned.

If many of the terrible social costs we feared in terms of civil disturbances and communal killings did not come to pass, one can ascribe it to the innate decency of the people, who saw in the interlopers ordinary people like themselves, with no sinister agenda to reduce the original settlers to a minority but people in search of jobs and livelihood. That charge must be laid at the door of our political parties, of various persuasions, who strove myopically to enlarge their political base. That the large-scale movements took place with the connivance of the political establishment is by now well-established.

I was in that region for too short a time for the usual feelings of the exile to manifest. Therefore, I can honestly say that I did not experience any cynicism or alienation due to that reason. I could see that what probably really divided us was the fact that we were part of the same country, shared a sense of shared destiny, and were subject to the same laws and rules, the same administration, the same corrupt officials and politicians, while the physical proximity in fact brought the differences into relief and heightened the realization of differences. I hope the stories recounted capture at least a part of that change in the narrator as he worked among the people of the region.

In a way, I probably got closer to the experience of the colonial administrators of the ICS (Indian Civil Services), as they arrived in a strange land to administer laws that were quite familiar to them, while the very laws and rules of behaviour were strange and at odds with the time-honoured practices and customs of the populace being governed.

The 'colonial' character of the administration was almost palpable, and was reflected in every transaction or interaction with the local people, in the backroom discussions among officials, in the decisions regarding key posts in the administration, indeed in every perception and nuance of the everyday minutiae of governance.

There was an elected government in Manipur, comprising entirely of people of that state. This government was the one I worked for, and whose ministers took the policy decisions that I was supposed, as a junior functionary, to implement. That these ministers misused their powers with impunity indicated, I suppose, a certain 'freedom' of action unhampered by restraints of any kind from Delhi. So in what sense do I say that there was a 'colonial' character to the governance?

First, the government was in a sense not really answerable to the people of the region. Of course, they were elected and removed from office periodically in the manner of their equally undistinguished counterparts on the mainland. But most of the effort of those in power appeared to be to get as much of the cake for themselves and their parties, while ensuring that the daily stream of grievances and petitions was attended to as far as possible. The revenues of the governments comprised mostly grants from Delhi, based on the criteria determined by the special conditions prevailing in the north-east, as well as the recommendations of the finance commissions. These grants – to be used for various development projects – were quite generous and were utilized through the agency of government departments and contractors who executed the work. So little of the money allocated for various purposes actually reached the ground that the state earned the name 'Money-pur', with corruption attaining levels not seen elsewhere. Delhi's approach appears to have been: let them do what they want, as long our interests are served. And what were those interests? Keeping the insurgency down to a simmer so that the borders were not threatened, and nothing developed into a full-fledged revolt. If the lack of interest in the quality of life of the people is not a colonial mindset, what is?

Second, the heavy deployment of the military and paramilitary forces in the north-east tends to be dismissed as something necessitated by the 'sensitive' borders. With China to the north, Myanmar to the east and Bangladesh to the west, that would appear to be a valid perception. But the heavy deployment of the CRPF, Assam Rifles, and battalions of other armed police units from distant states cannot be explained away that easily. When I was a young field officer, security was handled by the police with assistance from paramilitary units of the Assam Rifles, CRPF and BSF. A few years later, a full division of the army moved into Manipur. What had called for such a response from Delhi? I can only imagine this having been the result of a report put together by someone who had travelled down from Delhi, spent a few days there, and quickly come to the conclusion that the north-east was on the verge of being lost unless decisive action was taken.

The 'inner line' regulations covering much of the region – and almost the entire state of Manipur except the Central District – imposed curbs on the entry and movement of people from the rest of the country in those parts. The draconian AFSPA ensured that these forces were equipped with formidable powers to be used not against external threat, but against the people of the region. Even the battalions of the Manipur Rifles were composed mostly of people of Nepali descent, as were the battalions of the Assam

Rifles. The latter drew its officer cadre almost entirely from the Indian Army. So, the region in general, and Manipur in particular, was covered under a security blanket that was grossly excessive if viewed only in the context of an external threat.

Third, in those days, the senior echelons of the administration were drawn from other states, on the plea that Manipur, and presumably other north-eastern states as well, did not have enough officers qualifying to be selected to the IAS and IPS. Those few Manipuri officers that *were* in these services were mostly those who had joined the state administrative or police service, and were 'conferred' the IAS or IPS, presumably for having a political godfather. In the Brahminical tradition of the IAS, they were referred to as 'conferred', which left no one in doubt about their status! They anyway rarely got important posts, which were almost always reserved for those on deputation.

It would be reasonably correct to say that, given the presence of these three features of governance, one must inevitably come to the conclusion that the governance of Manipur in the 1970s was colonial in outlook and substance.

It appears that matters have not improved over the years, with the same mistakes being repeated by successive administrations. North Block continues to take an imperial view of north-eastern affairs, with the reports of regional satraps and viceroys sent from Delhi (mostly over-the-hill politicians) forming the basis of plans and actions. The front-line administration continues to flounder in a twilight zone where nothing is clear or familiar, where the writ of the government is often confined to motorable roads, and the status quo enforced by weapon-toting soldiers.

The melancholy truth is that we don't seem to have learnt from our mistakes yet. But things can be remedied still. There are so many people, both in and out of uniform, who have an excellent grasp of the real issues in the north-east, that it should be a relatively simple matter to get a few of them together to put together a credible plan to start undoing the damage of the past decades, and begin the process of healing the terrible wounds inflicted on civil society and indeed on a whole way of life and culture that is quite distinctive and adds so much to the colour and diversity of India. That is not going to bep an easy task, and will not be simply accomplished by withdrawing the army and other paramilitary units from that region. However, if we take into account the fact that the disgruntled population has valid grievances and that the men and women who are protesting are as eager to get back to their lives as any person, the problems of the region will cease to seem insurmountable. I do believe that a close and honest look at the ground realities of the region will help throw up the answer to the very tricky question of what needs to be done to remedy the situation. And I hope that this book becomes one of the instruments that enable these worthies to understand the region and its problems better.

Acknowledgements

First, I would like to thank my wife Vinita for egging me on to write this book. With her encouragement and persistence, she made sure that what started out as a fun exercise ended up as a book. Her faith in the book finding a good publisher never flagged, and she made sure that I did not abandon efforts to get it accepted by a reputed publisher and go ahead on my own.

I am grateful to my good friend Mini Krishnan who helped me understand the unfamiliar ways of publishing, and prepared me for the long and difficult process of finding a publisher. The fact that Mini felt that the book had merit meant a lot to me during the wait till the book was accepted by HarperCollins.

I owe a debt of gratitude to Ranjit Nair for suggesting the book to my publishers, and also for following up with them.

I thank Sarita Sunder and her business partner Ram Sinam for reading the early drafts and providing constructive criticism. Sarita designed and printed some copies of an early version of the book, which helped me send it to potential publishers. I am particularly grateful to Ram for offering his excellent photographs of the vistas and people of Manipur to be used in the book. I believe the reader will agree that they help give a whole new meaning to the descriptions strewn through the pages.

I am grateful to several friends who read early drafts of the book and offered their suggestions and comments. I would like to mention Lt Gen. (retd) Sushil Pillay, Arun M. Kumar, Poornima Kumar and Naved Masood from a small list of friends who gave me their frank comments and suggestions, some of which I tried to incorporate in the final draft.

To Arun I owe a special debt for his excellent suggestion for the title of the book. It was he who pointed out that the book is more than a collection of anecdotes about the north-east of India, that it is a meditation on issues concerning identity and nationhood that are being interrogated again forcefully today.

I am grateful to Prema Govindan for the comprehensive editing inputs that have gone into the making of the final draft. Since I went through every editing suggestion made by her, I was able to get an idea of the work involved in this exercise. Mr Krishan Chopra's read added the final polish that the book needed and I would like to thank him for it. I would also like to thank the other members of the HarperCollins team who were involved in the production of the book for their efforts and help.